Helmut Debelius
UNTERWASSERFÜHRER ROTES MEER
Fische

Liebe „Guris"

ein kleiner Vorgeschmack auf Ägypten. Für die Vorfreude.

Luzi & Hans

PS: freuen uns auf einen „Sansotonen" Urlaub!

Helmut Debelius

UNTERWASSER FÜHRER
Rotes Meer
Fische

Delius Klasing Verlag

Alle in diesem Buch enthaltenen Angaben, Daten, Ergebnisse usw. wurden von den Autoren nach bestem Wissen erstellt und von ihnen und vom Verlag sorgfältig überprüft. Gleichwohl können inhaltliche Fehler nicht vollständig ausgeschlossen werden. Daher erfolgen die gemachten Angaben, Daten, Ergebnisse usw. ohne jegliche Verpflichtung oder Garantie des Autors oder des Verlags. Weder die Autoren noch der Verlag übernehmen irgendeine Verantwortung und Haftung für etwaige inhaltliche Unrichtigkeiten.

Geschützte Warennamen und Warenzeichen werden nicht besonders gekennzeichnet. Aus dem Fehlen solcher Hinweise kann nicht geschlossen werden, daß es sich um freie Warennamen bzw. freie Warenzeichen handelt.

Bibliografische Information der Deutschen Nationalbibliothek
Die Deutsche Nationalbibliothek verzeichnet diese Publikation
in der Deutschen Nationalbibliografie;
detaillierte bibliografische Daten sind im Internet
über http://dnb.d-nb.de abrufbar.

Der Verlag macht darauf aufmerksam, daß dieses Buch bereits
in 6 Auflagen unter der ISBN 3-89594-021-6 angeboten wurde.

8. Auflage
ISBN 978-3-7688-1796-7
© by Verlag Stephanie Naglschmid, Stuttgart
Herausgegeben in der EDITION NAGLSCHMID

Herausgeber: Dr. Friedrich Naglschmid
Umschlaggestaltung: Buchholz / Hinsch / Hensinger, Hamburg
Titelfoto: Peter Nahke/MTi-Press
Zeichnungen: Stephanie Naglschmid/MTi-Press
Englische Übersetzung: William N. Weaver jr.
Druck: Kunst- und Werbedruck, Bad Oeynhausen
Printed in Germany 2009

Alle Rechte, insbesondere das Recht der Vervielfältigung und Verbreitung und der Übersetzung, vorbehalten. Kein Teil des Werkes darf in irgendeiner Form (durch Fotokopie, Mikrofilm oder ein anderes Verfahren) ohne schriftliche Genehmigung des Verlages reproduziert oder unter Verwendung elektronischer Systeme verarbeitet, vervielfältigt oder verbreitet werden.

Vertrieb: Delius Klasing Verlag, Siekerwall 21, D-33602 Bielefeld
Tel.: 0521/559-0, Fax: 0521/559-115
E-Mail: info@delius-klasing.de
www.delius-klasing.de

VORWORT

Das Rote Meer zählt durch seine interessante und nahezu einzigartige geologische Gestaltung zu den faszinierendsten Tauchgründen, die uns Menschen zugänglich sind. Einzigartig in seiner Zusammensetzung ist die Fauna dieses Meeres. Verlag, Herausgeber und Autor wollen diesen Unterwasserführer, der ausschließlich Biotopaufnahmen der vorgestellten Fischarten enthält, zugleich als Aufruf zum Schutz des Roten Meeres und seiner Lebewesen verstanden wissen. Wer in die Geheimnisse der Meere Einblick gewinnen konnte, wird begreifen und bereit sein, für den Schutz der Meere und ihrer Lebensformen einzutreten und somit auch die Lebensgrundlagen für uns Menschen zu erhalten.

Dr. Friedrich Naglschmid

FOREWORD

Due to its extraordinary geological situation the Red Sea ist one of the most fascinating diving areas in the world. All photographs of the animals described in this book have been taken directly in the reefs of the Red Sea. Publisher, editor and author want to present this special kind of underwater guide as an appeal to protect the coral reefs and their fantastic life. Those who have had a closer look at the secrets of the sea and the mystery of the sea life will understand and want to be engaged in the protection of the marine environment and its life forms, which is basic for human life.

Dr. Friedrich Naglschmid

SCHEMA EINES KNOCHENFISCHES
SCHEME OF A BONEFISH

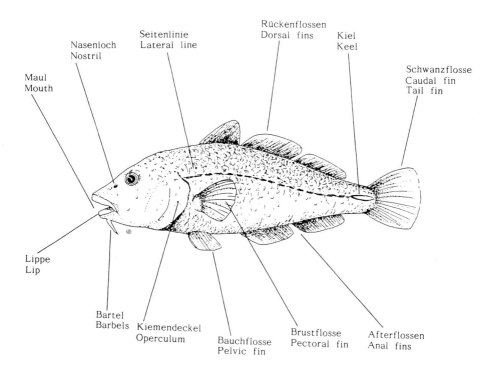

INHALT – CONTENTS

Vorwort – Foreword 5
Schema eines Knochenfisches – Scheme of a bonefish 6
Inhaltsverzeichnis – Contents 7
Einleitung – Preface 10
Küstenstruktur des Roten Meeres – 16
Structure of the Red Sea coastline
Gebrauchsanweisung – How to use this book 20
Übersichtskarte – Map of the Red Sea 22

Doktorfische – Surgeonfishes or Tangs 24

Zackenbarsche – Groupers  36

Kleine Barsche – Basslets 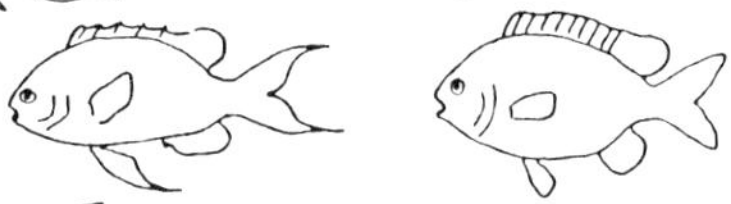 44

Barben – Goatfishes 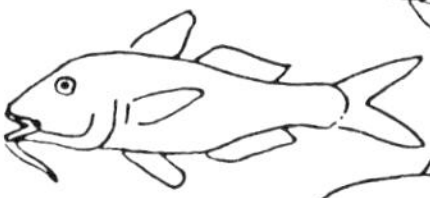 56

Große Lippfische – Big Wrasses 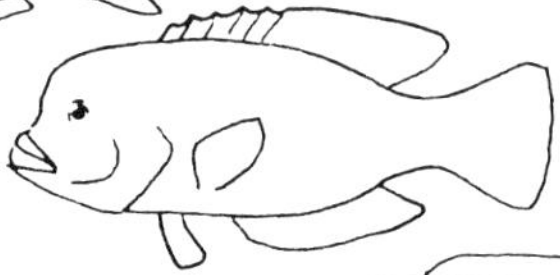 60

Kleine Lippfische – Small Wrasses 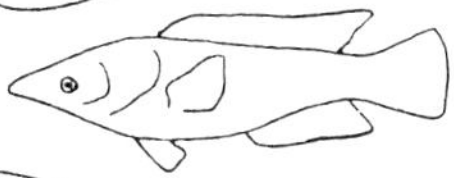 68

Papageienfische – Parrotfishes 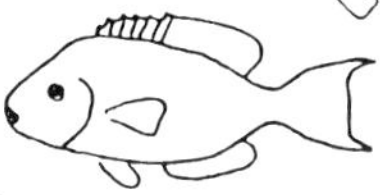 74

Muränen – Morays  78

Pfeifenfische – Pipefishes  82

Skorpionsfische – Scorpionfishes	88
Krokodilfische – Flatheads	92
Flügelroßfische – Seamoths	92
Eidechsenfische – Lizardfishes	94
Anglerfische – Frogfishes	94
Flötenfische – Cornetfishes	96
Welse – Eel Catfishes	96
Fledermausfische – Batfishes	98
Feilenfische – Filefishes	98
Kofferfische – Boxfishes	100
Blitzlichtfische – Flashlightfishes	100
Stachelmakrelen – Jacks	102
Barrakudas – Barracudas	106

Schnapper – Snappers	108
Brassen – Breams	112
Füsiliere – Fusiliers	112
Drückerfische – Triggerfishes	114
Kugelfische – Pufferfishes	120
Soldatenfische – Soldierfishes	126
Kaiserfische – Angelfishes	130
Falterfische – Butterflyfishes	138
Wimpelfische – Bannerfishes	148
Rochen – Rays	150
Haie – Sharks	156

Index Deutsch – Index German	164
Index Englisch – Index English	167
Index wissenschaftlich – Index scientific	170
Bildnachweis – Photo Credit	173
Literaturverzeichnis – Bibliography	174

EINLEITUNG

Meine Faszination für das Rote Meer hält mich nun schon mehr als zehn Jahre gefangen. Und je öfter ich zu diesem für Europäer naheliegendsten tropischen Meer reise, desto kürzer werden die Abstände der Wiederkehr. Der Kenner weiß es seit langem: Die Meeresfauna des Roten Meeres ist einmalig im Gesamtbereich des Indischen Ozeans. Mehr als zehn Prozent der Fischarten des Roten Meeres gibt es nur zwischen dem Suezkanal im Norden und dem Tor der Tränen (Bab-el-Mandab) im Süden. Als Taucher und

Eduard Rüppell

Schnorchler kann man diese Fischarten also weder bei den Malediven, noch um Indonesien oder in der Karibik sehen. Da die Unterwassersicht im Roten Meer im Jahresschnitt zudem weitaus besser als die aller bekannten Gebiete im Indik ist, macht es insbesondere dem Unterwasserfotografen und -filmer mehr Freude, hier den Fischreichtum und den üppigen Korallenwuchs zu dokumentieren. Beim Durchstöbern wissenschaftlicher Literatur über Fische bin ich immer wieder auf zwei Namen gestoßen, die für mich die eigentlichen Erforscher der Fischfauna des Roten Meeres gewesen sind und bis heute nicht übertroffen wurden:
Peter Forsskal (1732–1763) und **Eduard Rüppell** (1795–1884).
Hinter vielen lateinischen Fischnamen steht ihr Name oder ihr Namenskürzel. Dies bedeutet, daß sie diese Arten entdeckt und als erste beschrieben haben. Unter welchen Umständen das geschah, ist dermaßen fesselnd, daß ich jedem Rotmeerbesucher diese Reiseberichte nur empfehlen kann, die über oder von

beiden geschrieben wurden (siehe Literaturverzeichnis). Der schwedische Botaniker Forsskal war Teilnehmer einer sechsköpfigen Expedition, die im Auftrag des dänischen Königs 1761 Kopenhagen verließ, um „Arabia felix", das glückliche Arabien zu erforschen.
Das geheimnisvolle und bis dahin nahezu unbekannte Land Jemen war Ziel der Reise. Doch das Vorhaben stand unter einem schlechten Stern. Auf dem Weg durch die Türkei und Ägypten überschatteten unüberbrückbare Spannungen zwischen den Expeditionsteilnehmern den farbigen Alltag der Reise. Erst in Arabien selbst drängten drohende Gefahren alle persönlichen Mißhelligkeiten in den Hintergrund. Trotzdem wurde die Expedition zum katastrophalen Abenteuer. Als ihr letzter Überlebender, der deutsche Geometer Carsten Niebuhr nach sieben Jahren wieder in Kopenhagen eintrifft, kann er nur die Forschungsergebnisse seines Kollegen Forsskal mitbringen, der bereits im Jemen an Malaria verstorben war. Ihm verdanken wir letztendlich 58 Erstbeschreibungen von Rotmeerfischen, u. a. auch die vom für mich schönsten Kaiserfisch überhaupt, *Pomacanthus asfur*, populär Halbmondkaiser genannt.
Unter kaum weniger widrigen Umständen führte der deutsche Naturwissenschaftler Eduard Rüppell, Mitbegründer des Museums Senckenberg in Frankfurt am Main, finanziell unabhängig und in Eigenregie 1822 die erste von mehreren Reisen ans Rote Meer durch. Summiert man die veröffentlichten Sammlungsergebnisse seiner Fischuntersuchungen, so hat er während seiner Rotmeerreisen 175 neue Arten entdeckt. Bis jedoch die kunstgerecht aufbereiteten und naturecht gefärbten Hautpräparate der Rotmeerfische in Frankfurt ausgestellt werden konnten, wurde der sprachbegabte Forscher in politische Unruhen, Bürgerkriege und Raubüberfälle verwickelt und mußte dabei lebensgefährliche Lagen überstehen. Selbst auf der Rückreise nach Europa wurde er noch von Seeräubern gefangen genommen. Rüppell konnte seine Forschungen selbst auswerten und starb neunzigjährig als einer der bedeutendsten zoologischen Sammler seiner Zeit.
Alle Fischarten des Roten Meeres zusammen in einem Buch vorzustellen, ist auch heute noch ein schwieriges Unterfangen, zumal man ihre genaue Anzahl nur schätzen kann. Eine bestmögliche Auflistung der bisher geschätzten tausend Arten von Rotmeerfischen aus allen Tiefen wurde 1982 von dem israelischen Fischkundler Menachem Dor vorgenommen. Allerdings ist diese Aufstellung nicht illustriert. 1983 erschien dann das erste umfassend illustrierte Rotmeerfischbuch von dem amerikanischen Ichthyologen John E. Randall, der sich in seinem Buch „Red Sea Reef Fishes" auf riffgebunden lebende Fische beschränkt, aber immerhin 325 Arten vorstellt. Ein Buch, das Wissenschaftlern, Tauchern und Schnorchlern eine Bestimmungshilfe für die Fische gibt, die man im Riffbereich bis ca. 40 m Tiefe antreffen kann. Randalls vorbildliches systematisches Werk diente mir auch als Orientierung für dieses

Buch, allerdings wollte ich vermeiden, tote Fische abzubilden. Durch gemeinsame Reisen kenne ich Randalls wissenschaftliche Arbeitsweise, die gerade gefangenen und getöteten Fische so schnell wie möglich für ein Foto zu präparieren. Hauptaugenmerk wird dabei auf das Strecken der Flossen gerichtet, damit man die für die Bestimmung wichtige Anzahl der Flossenstrahlen genau abzählen kann. Eine Bestimmungsmethode, die für den Beobachter im Riff nicht nachzuvollziehen ist. Zudem verlieren die so behandelten Tiere oft ihre originäre Färbung. Um eine der Naturbeobachtung gerecht werdende Darstellung der Fische zu gewährleisten, sind sämtliche in diesem Buch abgebildeten Arten in ihrem natürlichen Lebensraum an den Riffen des Roten Meeres aufgenommen. So wie sie der Taucher und Schnorchler in den sonnendurchfluteten oberen Wasserzonen oder in größeren Tiefen, mit Kunstlicht beleuchtet, durch seine Taucherbrille sieht. Besonderen Wert habe ich darauf gelegt, kurzzeitige Riffbesucher wie Makrelen, Barrakudas oder auch Haie vorzustellen, die z. T. recht schwierig zu fotografieren sind, weil sie – und das trifft insbesondere auf Haie zu – dem tauchenden Menschen gegenüber sehr scheu sind.

Die Auswahl der Arten wurde den Worten eines Sprachführers gleich gewählt. So wie man sich fürs erste mit wenigen Worten verständigen kann, wurden entsprechend jeweils die Familien und Arten ausgewählt, denen man am häufigsten als Taucher unter Wasser begegnet. Ergänzt und erweitert wurde diese Auswahl durch Fische mit auffälliger Form, Färbung, Größe und Verhaltensweise. Apropos Größe: Aus eigener Erfahrung weiß ich, daß für den Rotmeertaucher der vorbeischwimmende Fisch nicht groß genug sein kann (!), so habe ich die wirklichen „Brocken" an Riffischen vollständig in das Buch aufgenommen, oft auch im Größenverhältnis zum Taucher oder anderen bekannten Fischen. Diese Auswahl zwang aber auch dazu, die liebenswerten Winzlinge wie Grundeln und Schleimfische innerhalb dieses Bandes zu übergehen. Hier empfiehlt sich die weiterführende und ergänzende Literatur, die im Literaturverzeichnis aufgeführt ist.

Die aus meiner Sicht mit 175 Fotos erlangte repräsentative Übersicht der im Tiefenbereich bis 50 m vorkommenden Fische wurde von den Ikan-Fotografen und mir an den meistbesuchten Tauchplätzen des Roten Meeres erlangt. Vollständig werden sogar die Doktor-, Drücker- und Kaiserfische erfaßt: Jede im Roten Meer schwimmende Art dieser Familien ist in diesem Buch abgebildet.

Meine Fotos entstanden vom Schiff des Veranstalters Udo Bönsel in der Bab-el-Mandab, von Aqaba/Jordanien (Basisleiter Björn van Daelen), von Jeddah/Saudi-Arabien (Basisleiter Hagen Schmid), von Sharm-el-Sheik/Ägypten (Basisleiter Rolf Schmidt) und von Hurghada/Ägypten (Basisleiter Rudi Kneip) ausgehend.

Helmut Debelius

PREFACE

My fascination for the Red Sea has held me in its grip for more than ten years now. And the more often I visit this tropical sea so easily accessible to Europeans the shorter the interval until my next return. The expert has known for a long time that within the whole Indian Ocean region, the fauna of the Red Sea ist the most unique. More than ten percent of the species of fish living in the ·Red Sea can only be found between the Suez Canal in the

Peter Forsskal

North and the „Gateway of Tears" (Bab-el-Mandab) in the South. These species of fish cannot be seen by diver or snorkler in the Maldives or Indonesia or in the Caribbean waters. Because the underwater visibility in the Red Sea is by far the best of any of the other well-known areas, and because of its abundance of fish and luxuriant growths of coral, underwater photographers and film-makers find it much more pleasant to document their subjects there. On my rummages through the scientific literature about fish, I continually come across the same two names who for me were always the real explorers of the fish fauna in the Red Sea. No one to this very day has ever been able to outdo **Peter Forsskal** (1732–1763) and **Eduard Rüppell** (1795–1884).

After many Latin fish names is either one of their names or its abbrevation. This means that they have discovered a particular species of fish and were the first to describe it. I can thoroughly recommend that visitors to the Red Sea area should, under any circumstances, read about the lives of these two explorers or read what they have written, since it is very fascinating indeed. The Swedish botanist Forsskal was a member of a six person expedition, who under contract to the Danish king left Copenhagen in 1761 to explore "Arabia

Felix", or "the fortunate land of Arabia". Their destination was the then unknown und mysterious land of Yemen. However, their plans seemed doomed from the beginning. Despite colourful and interesting surroundings all along the way, there was a continuous feeling of conflict and tension among the members of the expedition. In Arabia, however it was the outside pressure of threatening danger which pushed the personal animosities into the background. Nevertheless, the expedition was heading for some really diastrous adventures. The only survivor, the German surveyor Carsten Niebuhr, who made it back to Copenhagen, seven years later, only managed to bring back with him the results of the research of his colleague Forsskal, who had already died in Yemen of Malaria. It is Forsskal that we have to thank for being the first to describe 58 species of Red Sea fishes, especially what is for me the most beautiful angelfish of all, *Pomacanthus asfur*, commonly known as the "crescent Angelfish".

The German natural scientist Eduard Rüppell, co-founder of the Senckenberg Museum in Frankfurt, endured circumstances that were by no means less unpleasant when he undertook the first of several visits to the Red Sea in 1822, self-financed and self-organized. If one would take the time to put together all the research results of all his visits to the Red Sea, one would find out that he discovered a total of 175 different species. Before he was able to get to the task of preparing the Red Sea fishes for exhibition in Frankfurt by stuffing and painting them realistically, this linguistically gifted scientist was involved in political unrest, civil wars, and armed robbery, and lived in constant danger of his life. On his way back to Europe, he was even captured by a band of pirates and held prisoner. Rüppell was himself able to assess his research work and died in his nineties as one of the most famous zoologial collectors of his time. Today it is an extremely difficult task to depict all the species of fish from the Red Sea together in one book, since we can only guess at the actual number. The best listing of the thousand species of Red Sea fish found at all depths, has been put together by the Israeli fish expert Menachem Dor, but this listing is not illustrated. The first comprehensive illustrated Red Sea Fishes book appeared in 1983, written by the American ichthyologist John E. Randall. "Red Sea Reef Fishes" is limited to reef-dwelling fishes, but still introduces 325 species. This book gives scientists, divers and snorklers assistance in classifying the fishes they encounter around the reef down to a depth of 40 m. It is Randalls high quality systematic work that I used as my orientation for this book, but I wanted to avoid illustrating it with dead fish. From my travels together with Randall I know from his scientific working methods that one has to work very quickly indeed when preparing freshly collected and dead fish for photographing. Special attention has to be given to the way the fins are stretched so that the essential determination of the number of spines can be counted exactly. This method of determination, however, cannot be used by an underwater observer. Moreover, the creatures lose most of their original colours when handled in this manner. In order to give the nature observer a better idea of how the fishes look alive, all the pictures in this book were taken of species in their natural surroundings around the Red Sea reefs. They appear exactly as the divers or snorklers would see them through a diving mask, either in the sunlit upper waters or under artificial light down in the depths of the sea. I have made a special point of introducing the occasional reef visitors such as jacks, barracudas and also sharks, who are sometimes quite difficult to photograph, especially so the sharks, because they are very shy of divers.

The selection of the species in this book can be likened to the method of a language teacher. As a language teacher student would only understand a few words at the beginning, so is it the same with getting to know families and species of fish that the diver would soon recognize on sight, under water. Additions and expansions to this selection were made later on fish with eye-catching colours, size and behaviour patterns. Regarding size: Through my own experience I can honestly say, that for the Red Sea diver the fish can't be big enough! In this book I have picked out the real "big fellows", comparing their size against a diver or other well-known fish. The selection of fish in this edition, however, forced me to neglect the charming, tiny fish, such as Gobies and Blennies. In this connection, I would recommend the study of further supplementary literature listed by the author, in the bibliography. From my point of view the photographs which were shot by the IKAN photographers and myself in the most-visited diving areas of the Red Sea, are representative of the fish that can be found in the depths of up to 50 m. But more than that, the surgeon, trigger and angelfish families are completely documented: every species of these families swimming in the Red Sea are pictured in this book.

My photographs were taken from the vessel of the organiser Udo Bönsel around Bab-el-Mandab, off Aqaba, Jordan (Björn van Daelen's diving base), off Jeddah, Saudi Arabia (Hagen Schmid's diving base), off Sharm-el-Sheik, Egypt (Rolf Schmidt's diving base) and off Hurghada, Egypt (Rudi Kneip's diving base).

Helmut Debelius

KÜSTENSTRUKTUR DES ROTEN MEERES

Das Rote Meer nimmt eine Sonderstellung unter den Weltmeeren ein. Geologisch betrachtet gehört es zum syrisch-ostafrikanischen Grabensystem, welches sich im Tertiär einsenkte. Im Norden stellt der Bruchgraben des heutigen Golfes von Aqaba die Fortsetzung des von Jordantal, der Senke des Toten Meeres und Wadi Araba gebildeten Grabens dar. Im Süden endet das Rote Meer mit einer untermeerischen Schwelle, dem abessinischen Landriegel, im Bereich der heutigen Straße von Bab-el-Mandab, wodurch der Wasseraustausch mit dem Indopazifik stark eingeschränkt ist. So ist das Rote Meer, ozeanographisch betrachtet, ein Mittelmeer. Ähnlich wie das Hauptbecken besitzt auch der Golf von Aqaba nur einen schmalen Ausgang, die Straße von Tiran. Sie besteht aus einer Inselgruppe, mehreren mächtigen Riffen und einer untermeerischen Schwelle, die bis ca. 170 m an die Wasseroberfläche heraufreicht. Der Golf ist ca. 180 km lang, maximal 25 km breit und erreicht dabei eine enorme Tiefe von bis zu 1830 m. Seine Ränder werden von herausgehobenen Gebirgen gebildet, die in Küstennähe bis zu etwa 1000 m aufsteigen. Ihre Steilabfälle setzen sich auch unter Wasser fort und lassen nur wenig Platz für schmale, bis zu 50 m breite, abrupt abfallende Saumriffe. So wirkt der Golf von Aqaba wie ein riesiger Trog, der gegenüber dem Hauptbecken weitgehend isoliert ist. Im Gegensatz dazu stellt der Golf von Suez ein flaches Schelfmeer mit einer Tiefe von max. 80 bis 90 m dar.

Aufbau eines Lagunensaumriffes im Golf von Aqaba
Um einen Rifftyp zu beschreiben, sind Begriffe erforderlich, welche die Riffteile bezeichnen. Hierzu hat sich inzwischen eine eigene Riffnomenklatur entwickelt, wobei einzelne Riffstrukturen recht unterschiedlich bezeichnet werden. Für dieses Buch wurden hauptsächlich die von Mergner und Schuhmacher 1974 eingeführten Begriffe übernommen.

Rifflagune
Uferseitig, durch Erosion des Riffdaches metertief eingesenkt; eine meist sandige Stillwasserzone mit wenig Korallen.

Riffdach
Die flache Oberseite des Riffkörpers, der aus Korallenfels besteht. Oft leicht seewärts geneigt, erstreckt sich das Riffdach mehr oder weniger horizontal verlaufend bis zur Riffkante. Die Oberfläche ist meist durch Erosion kraterförmig zerfressen. Der Korallenbewuchs ist wegen der auslaufenden Brandungswellen und stärkerer Sedimentablagerungen gedrungen und recht spärlich.

Riffkrone
Seewärts gerichteter Teil des Riffdaches und höchste Erhebung des Riffes. Er ist oft so seicht, daß keine Fische mehr passieren können.

Riffkante
Schmaler Übergangsbereich zwischen Riffdach und Riffabhang. Starke Belastung durch Brandung, daher gedrungene Korallenwuchsformen. Oft mit Feuerkorallen bewachsen.

Riffabhang
Unterschiedlich steil abfallende Riffregion mit teilweise wächtenartig überhängender Riffkante, tiefen Löchern und Schluchten. Diese Zone ist stark mit Steinkorallen bewachsen.

Vorriff
Dem eigentlichen Riff seewärts vorgelagerter, aus Korallenpfeilern oder flächigem Bodenbewuchs bestehender Abschnitt. Er reicht bis in große Tiefen, wo er meist in eine Geröllhalde übergeht.

Riffpfeiler
Einzeln, meist auf sandiger Fläche isoliert stehender Korallenblock. Ihn findet man in allen Tiefen. Der Bewuchs an Steinkorallen ist artenreich.

STRUCTURE OF THE RED SEA COASTLINE

The Red Sea is part of the worlds greatest rift system, which includes the Jordan Valley with the Dead Sea and the East African Great Rift Valley. The Red Sea exceeds 2000 meters in depth but it is linked to the Indian Ocean by a shallow water zone, the sill at Bab-el-Mandab, which is little more than a hundred meters deep. This prevents major circulation between the Indian Ocean and the Red Sea. Thus this sea forms a "Mediterranean Sea" characterized by its isolation and water regime. A very similar situation exists in the Gulf of Aqaba, which is separated from the Red Sea by the straits of Tiran, a narrow passage about 170 m deep. There is a group of islands with considerable reefs close to the of the surface water. The Gulf of Aqaba is 180 km long, 14–25 km wide and almost 1830 m deep. On either side, beyond the shoreline, barren mountains rise to heights of approximately 1000 m. Because of this, the Gulf of Aqaba looks like a deep through, in contrast to the shallow basin of the Gulf of Suez with a depth of 80 to 90 m. The coral reefs form a fringing belt close to the shore.

Structure of a fringing lagoonar reef in the Gulf of Aqaba
To describe a distinct reef type you need some terms for the different zones of a reef. We use a slightly modified version of the nomenclature of Mergner and Schuhmacher published 1974 (see references).

Reef Lagoon
A deeply eroded zone of the reef just below the shoreline. Its bottom is covered with rubble and sand. The water often becomes quite warm, and there is little coral growth.

Reef Flat
The upper horizontal surface of the reef. It is built up of dead coral rock, with depp holes and caves eroded by the effects of water action. Due to the breaking of the waves in this zone, the corals are usually stumpy and sparse.

Reef Crest
The seaward pard of the reef flat representing the highest point of the reef. This zone ist often too shaloow for fish to cross. There are often many organ-pipe corals *(Tubipora musica)*.

Reef Edge
A narrow zon beyond the reef crest. When exposed to the surf the corals are very stumpy. Typical are the large colonies of fire corals *(Millepora dichotoma)*.

Reef Slope
The reef slope is usually steep and occasionally overhanging, with deep caves and canyons. Its upper part is generally the zone of greatest coral growth. Here are massive banks of mountain corals (Porites) or many species of staghorn corals (Acropora) forming more or less extended tables, umbrellas and plates. In the lower part there are often small terraces of bare coral rocks or sandy bottom.

Forereef
The forereef consists of a gradually sloping flat area with a mixture of sand, mud and coral rubble. It is covered by bizzarly shaped coral heads or pillars.

Reef Pillars
Single pillar-like knolls at a distance of from twenty to serveral hundred meters from the reef slope. They reach close to the surface and have their own very rich reef-edge communities.

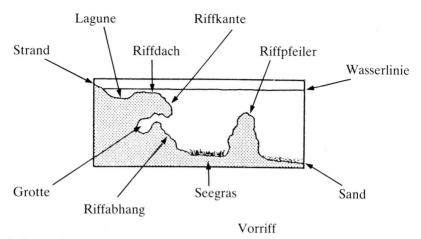

Gebrauchsanweisung

Dieses Buch erleichtert auf mehrfache Weise die Bestimmung von Fischen des Roten Meeres. Zunächst kann eine Grobeinordnung an Hand des Konturschlüssels ab Seite 7 vorgenommen werden. Man wählt die entsprechende Skizze für den zu bestimmenden Fisch und schlägt die dazu angegebene Seite auf. Dort findet man eine kurze Beschreibung der Fischfamilie, welche der Konturskizze zugeordnet ist. Hier kann überprüft werden, ob der eingeschlagene Weg stimmt. Wenn nicht, dann sollte man wieder zurück zu den Konturtafeln gehen und eine neue Wahl treffen.

Stimmen die beschriebenen Merkmale überein, dann kann mit Hilfe der Fotos und der gegenüberliegenden Beschreibung die Fischart oder zumindest die Gattung bestimmt werden. Auch Standort und Tiefenangaben sind oft wichtige Hilfsmittel für die Identifizierung einer Art; sie sind gut überschaubar in Form von Piktogrammen dargestellt. Umgekehrt können mit Hilfe der Piktogramme die angesprochenen Fische unter Wasser schneller aufgefunden werden. Die schwarzen Pfeile in den Riffskizzen weisen den Weg zu den bevorzugten Standorten dieser Fischarten. Ein dunkler Kreis bedeutet, daß die Fische in der vorgestellten Form (Foto) nur nachts anzutreffen sind, ein halbschattierter Kreis bedeutet Tag und Nacht, ein heller Kreis Tag. Das letzte Symbol, ein senkrechter Pfeil, erklärt die Tiefe, ab der sich die beschriebene Fischart in der Regel aufhält. Die einzelnen Riffabschnitte werden am Ende der Einleitung erklärt. Im Text sind ergänzend zu den Piktogrammen und Farbfotos wesentliche Merkmale, Verhaltensweisen oder Besonderheiten der jeweiligen Art erläutert.

Das Literaturverzeichnis auf Seite 174 soll dem engagierten Leser die Suche nach ausführlicheren Beschreibungen erleichtern. Das Namensregister, ab Seite 164, erlaubt ein rasches Auffinden der Beschreibung und Abbildung der Fischarten, deren Namen man schon kennt.

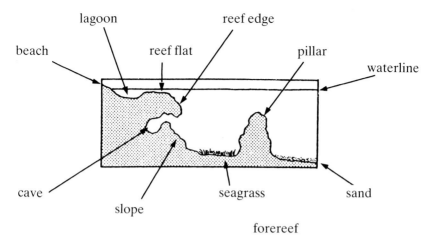

How to use this book

This book is intended to serve as a guide to the identification of the fishes of the Red Sea. The species described represent only a small part the total fauna but are the most common you will find on your underwater trip. To identify an unfamilar animal first turn to page 7 which shows drawings of typical examples of the different groups of fishes. Then simply compare the drawings with the fishes you have seen. Your turn to the text where that group of fishes is discussed. It the characteristics described agrees with your specimen, turn to the photographic plates, if not go back to page 7 and take another choice.

Facing each illustration is a legend page that explains the species. Arrows in reef pictogrammes help you to find their habitats. The daily activity of the animals on the photos is demonstrated by differently shadowed circles. Totally shadowed corresponded to night active, half shadowed to day and night and blank corresponds to the animals shape and behaviour during daytime. The last symbol, a vertical arrow, describes the upper depth limit of the species distribution. The reef pictogramme is discussed at the end of the introduction. The references at page 174 help you to find more detailed descriptions in the literature. Finally, an index of the species names, page 164, fasten your search for the species you now.

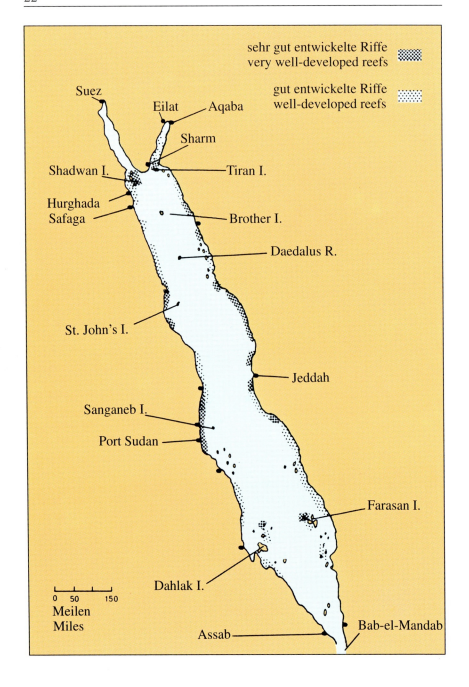

Der berühmteste Tauchplatz im Roten Meer:
Ras Muhamed

DOKTORFISCHE SURGEONFISHES OR TANGS
ACANTHURIDAE

Die an den Riffen des Roten Meeres allgegenwärtigen Doktorfische sind leicht an einem typischen Merkmal zu erkennen. Sie tragen an der Wurzel ihrer Schwanzflosse ihre „Waffe", entweder einen klappbaren Dorn oder zwei feststehende Klingen auf beiden Körperseiten. Aufgrund dieser Unterschiede wurde die Familie Acanthuridae auch unterteilt. Die Unterfamilie Acanthurinae trägt zum Teil mit Warnfarben ausgestattete Dorne, die sie bei Gefahr ausklappt und zum Aufschlitzen des Gegners benutzt. Wichtig: Das geschieht nicht willkürlich, da es keine Muskelverbindung vom Dorn zum Fischkörper gibt. Der Dorn springt aber bei Konkavwendung der Schwanzflosse im Winkel von 80 Grad nach vorn heraus. Die Unterfamilie Nasinae benutzt ihre feststehenden Klingen in ähnlicher Weise. Insbesondere bei älteren Tieren sind sie lang, messerscharf und daher wirkungsvoll. Doktorfische ernähren sich hauptsächlich von Algen, einige Arten nehmen auch Plankton aus dem freien Wasser. Sie sind wendige Schwimmer und erreichen ausgewachsen eine Länge von 75 cm (Arten der Gattung *Naso*).

The ever-present surgeonfishes in the Red Sea reefs are easy to recognize by a typical marking. They bear their "weapon" at the base of the tail fin: either a folding spine or two rigid, sharp blades (or keels) on each side of the body. The family Acanthuridae is also subdivided on the basis of these differences. Part of the sub-family Acanthurinae has equipped spines with warning coloration. These are erected when danger threatens, and used to slash the opponent. Important: this is not a voluntary action, as there is no muscle connection from the spine to the body. With a concave bend of the tail fin, however, the spine flips open to a forward angle of 80 degrees. The sub-family Nasinae uses its rigid blades in a similar way. Especially on older specimens they are long, razor-sharp, and therefore effective. Surgeonfishes graze primarily on algae; some species also feed on plankton in the open water. They are maneuverable swimmers, and species of the genus *Naso* attain a length oft 75 cm when fully grown.

Ein Paar Brauner Segelflossendoktorfische schwimmt über einem Rotmeerriff.
A pair of brown sailfintangs swims above a Red Sea Reef.

DOKTORFISCHE SURGEONFISHES ACANTHURIDAE

Brauner Segelflossendoktor Brown Sailfintang *Zebrasoma desjardini*
Blauer Segelflossendoktor Blue Sailfintang *Zebrasoma xanthurum*

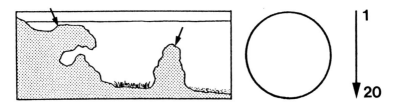

Doktorfische der Gattung *Zebrasoma* tragen überdurchschnittlich große Rücken- und Afterflossen, die sie bei Gefahr gerne aufstellen. Die segelartig ausgezogenen Flossen lassen diese Doktoren hoch und rund erscheinen. Besonders *Zebrasoma*-Jungfische wirken mit aufgestellten Flossen mehr als doppelt so groß. Im Roten Meer gibt es zwei Arten. Der Braune Segelflossendoktor lebt zwar auch im Indopazifik, doch fehlen ihm dort die Punkte auf der unteren Körperhälfte. Während diese Art gerne paarweise schwimmt, sieht man den Blauen Segelflossendoktor besonders im südlichen Roten Meer in kleinen Schulen. Bei beiden sind die Dorne farblich kaum sichtbar.

Surgeonfishes of the genus *Zebrasoma* have larger-then-average dorsal and anal fins, which they readily erect when threatened. When the saillike fins are extended they make the tangs look deep and round. Especially the young *Zebrasomas* look more than twice as large when they raise their fins. In the Red Sea there are two species. Though the brown sailfin tang also lives in the Indo-Pacific, the spots on the lower part of the body are absent there. While this species likes to swim in pairs, the blue sailfin tang is seen in small schools, especially in the southern Red Sea. The spines of both species are hardly visible by their coloration.

| Brauner Segelflossendoktor | Brown sailfintang | *Zebrasoma desjardini* |
| Blauer Segelflossendoktor | Blue sailfintang | *Zebrasoma xanthurum* |

DOKTORFISCHE SURGEONFISHES ACANTHURIDAE

Schwarzer Doktorfisch	Black tang	*Acanthurus gahhm*
Brauner Doktorfisch	Brown tang	*Acanthurus nigrofuscus*
Borstenzahndoktor	Bristletooth tang	*Ctenochaetus striatus*

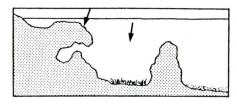 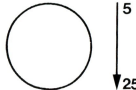

5
25

Nur eine Art der Doktorfischgattung *Ctenochaetus* gibt es im Roten Meer, allerdings nicht sehr attraktiv. Wie ihr populärer Name sagt, kann der Borstenzahndoktor große veralgte Flächen mit beweglichen Zähnen abraspeln.

In the Red Sea there is only one species of the surgeonfish genus *Ctenochaetus*, though not a very appealing one. As its popular name indicates, the bristletooth tang can scrape off large algae-covered surfaces with its movable teeth.

Borstenzahndoktor   Bristletooth tang   *Ctenochaetus striatus*

Schwarzer Doktorfisch   Black tang   *Acanthurus gahhm*

Brauner Doktorfisch   Brown tang   *Acanthurus nigrofuscus*

DOKTORFISCHE SURGEONFISHES ACANTHURIDAE

Sohaldoktorfisch Sohaltang *Acanthurus sohal*

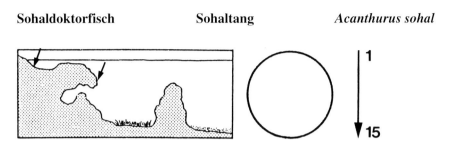

Der farbigste Doktorfisch seiner Gattung ist der Sohaldoktorfisch, insbesondere, wenn man ihn mit dem braunen oder schwarzen Doktorfisch vergleicht. Er macht deutlich auf seine „Waffe", den orangefarbenen Dorn am Schwanzstiel, aufmerksam und setzt sie auch als aggressive Art häufig ein. Der Sohaldoktor ist ein typischer Rotmeerfisch und ein sehr beweglicher Schwimmer. Auf dem Riffdach sieht man ihn in Schulen, in Wracks aber eher als Einzelgänger. Während zum Beispiel der schwarze Doktorfisch als Schwarmfisch gerne treibendes Plankton im freien Wasser frißt, bevorzugt der Sohaldoktorfisch auf dem sonnendurchfluteten Riff gewachsene Algenkost. Von den mit Dornen bewaffneten Rotmeerdoktorfischen wird er mit 40 cm Länge am größten.

The most colorful tang of its genus is the sohaltang, especially when one compares it with the brown or black tang. It clearly draws attention to its "weapon", the orange-colored spine on the base of the tail, and as an agressive species, uses it frequently. The sohal is a typical Red Sea fish and a very agile swimmer. On the reefflats they are seen in schools, but in wrecks more likely as solitaries. While the black tang, for example, as a schooling fish prefers to feed o drifting plankton in the open water, the sohal prefers the algae growing on the sunlit reef. Of all the Red Sea surgeonfishes armed with spines, this is the largest, with a length of 40 cm.

Sohaldoktorfisch Sohaltang *Acanthurus sohal*

DOKTORFISCHE SURGEONFISHES ACANTHURIDAE

Naso elegans Yellowspinetang *Naso lituratus*

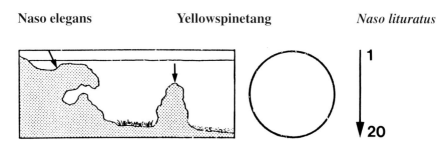

Doktorfische der Gattung *Naso* tragen je zwei feste Klingen an der Schwanzwurzel. Der Gelbklingendoktorfisch ist eine Art, die deutlich auf ihre Waffen hinweist. Sie trifft man mehr paarweise, selten im Schwarm an.

Tangs of the genus *Naso* have two rigid keels on the base of the tail. The yellowspinetang is a species which clearly displays its weapons. They are seen in pairs, seldom in schools.

Langnasendoktorfisch **Longnosetang** *Naso brevirostris*

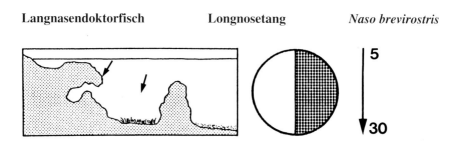

Als Einzelgänger sieht man im Roten Meer den Langnasendoktorfisch. Sein Hornfortsatz reicht weit über sein Maul hinaus.

As solitary specimens the longnosetang are seen in the whole Red Sea. Its horny appendix reaches a big length above its mouth.

| Gelbklingendoktorfisch | Yellowspinetang | *Naso lituratus* |
| Langnasendoktorfisch | Longnosetang | *Naso brevirostris* |

DOKTORFISCHE SURGEONFISHES ACANTHURIDAE

Kurznasendoktorfisch **Shortnosetang** *Naso unicornis*
Blauklingendoktorfisch **Bluespinetang** *Naso hexacanthus*

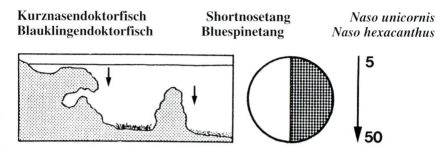

Auf dieser Doppelseite sieht man die Doktorfische, die im Roten Meer die größten Schwärme bilden: Kurznasendoktorfische und Blauklingendoktorfische. Auch sie leben von benthischen Algen, aber auch von Blattalgen wie Sargassum.

On these two pages are tangs which form the largest schools: shortnose tangs and bluespine tangs. They, too, live on benthic algae, but also on leafy algae such as Sargassum.

Kurznasendoktorfisch Shortnosetang *Naso unicornis*

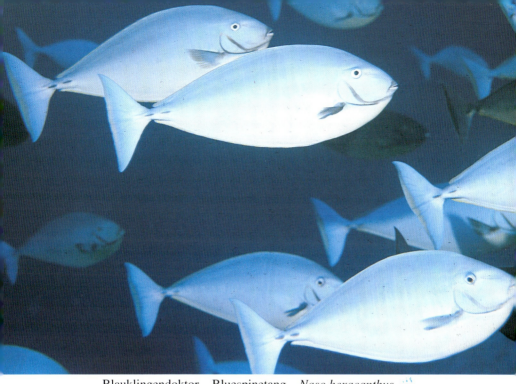

Blauklingendoktor   Bluespinetang   *Naso hexacanthus*

Balzendes Paar Blauklingendoktoren   Courting pair bluespinetangs

ZACKENBARSCHE   GROUPERS   SERRANIDAE

Welcher Taucher liebt sie nicht, die Zackenbarsche der Familie Serranidae? „Zackis", wie sie gerne populär genannt werden, beeindrucken durch ihren kompakten, wuchtigen Körper, den sie zur Jagd auf Fische und Krebstiere mit der überdimensionalen Schwanzflosse schlagartig antreiben können. Sonst sieht man die zumeist versteckt lebenden Raubfische eher langsam am Riff entlang gleiten. Die im Roten Meer lebenden Zackenbarsche werden bis zu 200 cm lang.

What diver doesn't love these groupers of the family Serranidae? Usually living in concealment, these predators have impressively compact, massive bodies, which they can suddenly propel with their oversized tail fins when hunting crustaceans and other fish. They are otherwise seen slowly gliding along the reef. Groupers of the Red Sea grow to a length of 200 cm.

Mondflossenzackenbarsch   **Lunartail grouper**   *Variola louti*
Malabarzackenbarsch   **Malabar grouper**   *Epinephelus malabaricus*

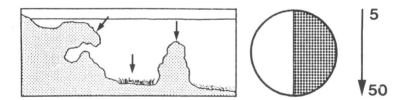

Zwei im Roten Meer recht häufige Zackenbarsche sind hier abgebildet. Sie streifen auch tagsüber regelmäßig über das Korallenriff oder stehen still im freien Wasser davor. Der Malabarzackenbarsch wird gerade von einem Putzerlippfisch geputzt. Er jagt gerne im trüben Wasser.

Here are two groupers quite common in the Red Sea. They also cruise over the coral reef during the day, or hang motionless in the open water in front of the reef. The Malabar grouper is being cleaned by a cleaner wrasse. It likes to hunt in murky water.

Mondflossenzackenbarsch   Lunartail grouper   *Variola louti*

Malabarzackenbarsch   Malabar grouper   *Epinephelus malabaricus*

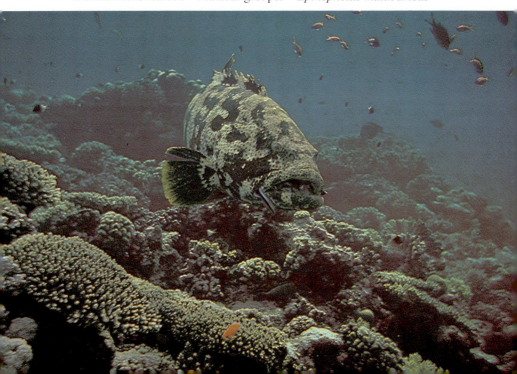

ZACKENBARSCHE GROUPERS SERRANIDAE

Rotmaulzackenbarsch Redmouth grouper *Aethaloperca rogaa*

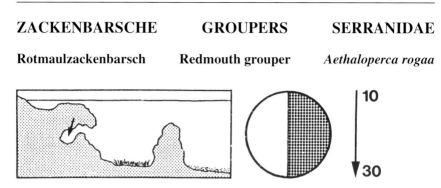

Sehr versteckt in den Riffen des Roten Meeres lebt auch der Rotmaulzackenbarsch. Man findet ihn in Höhlen oder unter dunklen Überhängen. Der oft nur als Schatten erkennbare, dunkelbraun gefärbte Fisch trägt im Jugendkleid eine weiße Abgrenzung an der Schwanzflosse.

The redmouth grouper lives quite hidden away in the reefs of the Red Sea. It is found in caves or under dark overhangs. The dark brown fish, often only recognizable as a shadow, has as a juvenile a white margin on the tail fin.

Riesenzackenbarsch **Giant Grouper** *Epinephelus tukula*

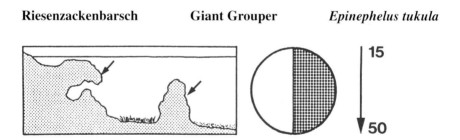

In allen Meeren der Erde, so auch im Roten Meer, findet der geduldige Beobachter den Riesenzackenbarsch. Allerdings gibt es hier Gegenden, wo er auch von tauchenden Wissenschaftlern noch nie gesehen wurde. Mit Sicherheit lebt diese Art an der ägyptischen Küste, sogar in kleineren Rudeln zusammen. Er kann eine Länge von 200 cm erreichen.

In the Red Sea, as in every other sea on earth, the patient observer will find the giant grouper. There are, however, areas here where it has never been seen by scientist divers. This species definitely inhabits the Egyptian coast, moreover in small groups. It can reach a length of 200 cm.

Rotmaulzackenbarsch   Redmouth grouper   *Aethaloperca rogaa*

Riesenzackenbarsch   Giant grouper   *Epinephelus tukula*

ZACKENBARSCHE   GROUPERS   SERRANIDAE

Juwelenzackenbarsch   **Jewelgrouper**   *Cephalopholis miniata*
Braunfleckenzackenbarsch   **Greasy grouper**   *Epinephelus tauvina*
Baskenmützenzackenbarsch   **Blacktip grouper**   *Epinephelus fasciatus*

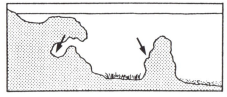 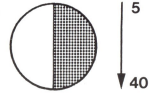

Die kleinwüchsigen Zackenbarsche sind auf dieser Doppelseite abgebildet. Farbenprächtig ist insbesondere der Juwelenzackenbarsch, dessen verschiedene Farbvarianten links unten und rechts oben erkennbar sind. Der Baskenmützenzackenbarsch wird gegenüber Tauchern handzahm.

The smaller groupers are pictured on these two pages. The jewel grouper is especially colourful, with colour variations recognizable below, left and above, right. The blacktip grouper can become quite tame with divers.

Juwelenzackenbarsch   Jewelgrouper   *Cephalopholis miniata*

| Braunfleckenzackenbarsch | Greasy grouper | *Epinephelus tauvina* |
| Baskenmützenzackenbarsch | Blacktip grouper | *Epinephelus fasciatus* |

ZACKENBARSCHE   GROUPERS   SERRANIDAE

Summanazackenbarsch   **Summana grouper**   *Epinephelus summana*
Leopardenzackenbarsch   **Leopard grouper**   *Plectropomus marisrubi*

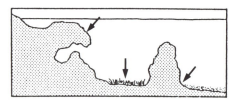 

Prächtige Exemplare ihrer Familie sind die 100 cm lang wachsenden Leopardenzackenbarsche, die es in verschiedenen Farbvariationen gibt. Sie streifen meist allein umher.

The 100 cm long leopard groupers are magnificent examples of their family. Occuring with colour variations, they usually cruise alone.

Summanazackenbarsch   Summana grouper   *Epinephelus summana*

Leopardenzackenbarsch   Leopard grouper   *Plectropomus marisrubi*

Dieselbe Art mit anderem Farbkleid   Same species with different colour

KLEINE BARSCHE BASSLETS SERRANIDAE

Verschiedene Familien Various families

Unter dieses Kapitel fallen Barschfamilien, deren Arten dem Beobachter vornehmlich durch ihre Farbenprächtigkeit auffallen. Allerdings werden die „Kleinen Barsche" nicht länger als 15 cm.

In this chapter are the bass families whose species are notable chiefly for their range of brilliant colours. The basslets do not grow longer than 15 cm, however.

ANEMONENFISCHE ANEMONEFISHES
POMACENTRIDAE

Rotmeeranemonenfisch Red sea anemonefish *Amphiprion bicinctus*

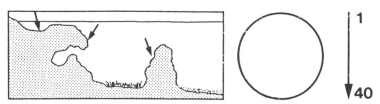

Anemonen- oder Clownsfische leben im gesamten Indopazifik in Symbiose mit nesselnden Aktinien, populär Anemonen genannt. Von den 25 Arten der Clownsfische kommt aber nur eine im Roten Meer vor, *Amphiprion bicinctus*. Meist trifft man Anemonenfische paarweise in ihrem Wirtstier an. Mit etwas Glück entdeckt man aber auch im Roten Meer Anemonenfelder, die von Unmengen von Anemonenfischen bewohnt werden.

Anemonefishes, or clownfishes, live in the entire Indo-Pacific in symbiosis with stinging Actinaria, populary called anemones. Of the 25 species of anemonefishes, only one is found in the Red Sea: *Amphiprion bicinctus*. One use usually encounters anemonefishes in pairs among their hosts. With luck one can also discover fields of anemones in the Red Sea which are inhabited by enormous quantities of these fishes.

RIFFBARSCHE
POMACENTRIDAE
DAMSELFISHES

Preußenfisch	Banded damsel	*Dascyllus aruanus*
Grüner Riffbarsch	Green damsel	*Chromis viridis*

Diese kleinen wendigen Riffbewohner sind so schmal, daß sie Schutz in den vielfältigen Verästelungen der Steinkoralle finden. Dort leben sie schwarmweise und verlassen so auch ihren Unterschlupf, um gemeinsam vorbeitreibendes Plankton aus dem Wasser zu erhaschen. Große Raubfische wie Makrelen oder Schnapper starten dabei immer wieder Überraschungsangriffe, um sich einen kleinen Riffbarsch einzuverleiben. Die einzelnen Korallenblöcke werden artspezifisch besiedelt, man duldet also keine andere Riffbarschart im gleichen „Wohnblock" oder mischt sich mit ihnen. Die meistverbreiteten Arten im Roten Meer sind hier einschließlich des schwarzen Dreifleck-Riffbarsches (auf Seite 45 in der Nähe der Anemonenfische) abgebildet.

These agile little reef-dwellers are so slender that they find protection in the multiple branchings of the stone corals. There they live in schools, and leave their hiding places together in order to catch plankton which is drifting past. At such times, large predators such as jacks or snappers start surprise attacks in order to catch little damselfishes. Each coral head is inhabited by a single species; no other species of damselfish is tolerated in the same "block of flats", and no mixing is allowed. The most widespread species in the Red Sea are pictured here, including the domino (on page 45 near the anemonefish).

Preußenfisch   Banded damsel   *Dascyllus aruanus*

Grüner Riffbarsch   Green damsel   *Chromis viridis*

FAHNENBARSCHE   FLAG BASSLETS   ANTHIIDAE

Haremsfahnenbarsch   Harem flag basslet   *Pseudanthias squamipinnis*
Streifenfahnenbarsch   Striped flag basslet   *Pseudanthias taeniatus*
Heemstrafahnenbarsch   Heemstra flag basslet   *Pseudanthias heemstrai*

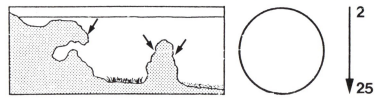

Die Häufigkeit von Fahnenbarschen wird im Roten Meer von keiner anderen Familie übertroffen. Sie bevölkern zu Tausenden alle Riffhänge. 1977 konnte ich mit dem Foto des *Pseudanthias heemstrai* erstmals eine dritte Art in einer Taucherzeitschrift vorstellen. Bisher waren nur zwei Arten bekannt.

The flag basslets occur in the Red Sea in a frequency not exceeded by any other family. They populate all the reef slopes by thousands. In 1977 I was able with the photo of the *Pseudanthias heemstrai* to introduce a third species for the first time in a divers' magazine. Up to then only two species were known.

Haremsfahnenbarsch   Harem flag basslet   *Pseudanthias squamipinnis* ♂

| Streifenfahnenbarsch | Striped flag basslet | *Pseudanthias taeniatus* ♂ |
| Heemstrafahnenbarsch | Heemstra flag basslet | *Pseudanthias heemstrai* ♂ |

ZWERGBARSCHE PYGMY BASSLETS
PSEUDOCHROMIDAE

Olivenzwergbarsch   Olive pygmy basslet   *Pseudochromis olivaceus*
Fridmans Zwergbarsch   Fridman's pygmy basslet   *Pseudochromis fridmani*
Springers Zwergbarsch   Springer's pygmy basslet   *Pseudochromis springeri*

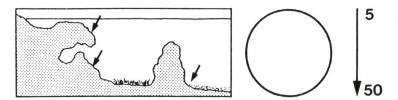

Gerade im Roten Meer kommen Zwergbarsche vor, die es sonst nirgendwo gibt. Sie werden zwar nicht länger als 10 cm, sollten aber durch ihre zum Teil brillante Färbung dem Beobachter im Riff auffallen.

Just in the Red Sea are pygmy basslets that do not occure elsewhere. Although they are no longer than 10 cm here, they should be conspicuous to the reef observer by their often brilliant coulouration.

Olivenzwergbarsch   Olive pygmy basslet   *Pseudochromis olivaceus*

Fridmans Zwergbarsch   Fridman's pygmy basslet   *Pseudochromis fridmani*

Springers Zwergbarsch   Springer's pygmy basslet   *Pseudochromis springeri*

BÜSCHELBARSCHE　　HAWKFISHES　　CIRRHITIDAE

Langnasenbüschelbarsch　　Longnose hawkfish　　*Oxycirrhites typus*

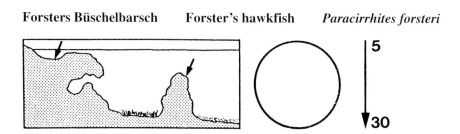

Wie unterschiedlich gebaut die Arten der Büschelbarschfamilie sein können, zeigen die im Roten Meer am häufigsten vorkommenden Arten. Bewegungslos in einer Hornkoralle lauernd, schnappt der Langnasenbüschelbarsch nach vorbeitreibenden Krebstieren im Plankton. Diese Art bewohnt gerne schwarze Korallen in tieferen Zonen.

The various species of the hawkfish family can have quite divergent forms, as seen by these most common species from the Red Sea. The longnose hawkfish, lurking motionless in a horny coral, snatches the crustaceans drifting past in the plankton. This species prefers to inhabit black corals in the deeper zones.

Forsters Büschelbarsch　　Forster's hawkfish　　*Paracirrhites forsteri*

Forsters Büschelbarsch dagegen hockt auch im sonnendurchfluteten Riff wie ein Wächter auf Korallenblöcken und greift blitzschnell kleinere vorbeischwimmende Fische an. Aufgrund seines bulligen Körpers ist er kein ausdauernder Schwimmer.

Forster's hawkfish, on the other hand, also crouches on coral heads in the sunlit reef like a sentry, and with lightning speed seizes smaller fish that swim past. Because of its stocky body it does not have much endurance as a swimmer.

Langnasenbüschelbarsch   Longnose hawkfish   *Oxycirrhites typus*

Forsters Büschelbarsch   Forster's hawkfish   *Paracirrhites forsteri*

MIRAKELBARSCHE DEVIL BASSLETS PLESIOPIDAE

Augenfleckmirakelbarsch Comet Basslet *Calloplesiops altivelis*

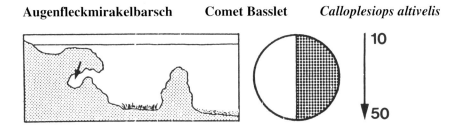

Sehr versteckt leben Mirakelbarsche. Sie tragen ungewöhnlich große Flossen, insbesondere die Schwanzflosse nimmt ein Drittel des Körpers ein. Ihr schönster Vertreter ist der Augenfleckmirakelbarsch.

Devil basslets live very secretively. They have unusually large fins; especially the tail fin makes up a third of the overall length. The most beautiful member of the family is the comet basslet.

SEIFENBARSCHE SOAPFISHES GRAMMISTIDAE

Goldstreifenseifenbarsch Goldstriped soapfish *Grammistes sexlineatus*

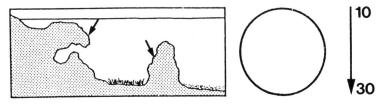

Ihren populären Namen erhielt diese Fischfamilie wegen der Fähigkeit, bei Gefahr einen giftigen Schleim abzusondern. Es wurde schon beobachtet, daß gerade verschluckte Seifenbarsche wieder unversehrt vom Freßfeind ausgespuckt wurden.

This fish family received its popular name for its ability to produce a toxic mucus when threatened. Observations have been made of soapfish being expelled again unharmed right after being swallowed by a predator.

Augenfleckmirakelbarsch   Comet basslet   *Calloplesiops altivelis*

Goldstreifenseifenbarsch   Goldstriped soapfish   *Grammistes sexlineatus*

BARBEN GOATFISHES MULLIDAE

Gelbsattelbarbe **Yellowsaddle goatfish** *Parupeneus cyclostomus*

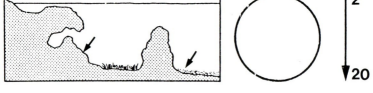

Das auffälligste Merkmal dieser auch im Roten Meer häufigen Fischfamilie sind die Barteln unter dem Kinn. Oft sieht man sie auf der Suche nach freßbaren Wirbellosen im Sand wühlen, sie benutzen aber auch die Barteln, um kleine Fische aus engen Korallenverstecken herauszupeitschen und sie dann zu fressen. Barben werden 50 cm lang.

The most striking feature of this numerous fish family in the Red Sea is the barbels on their chins. They are often seen grubbing in the sand for edible invertebrates. They also use the barbels to drive out smaller fish from narrow crevices in the coral so they can be eaten. Goatfishes reach a length of 50 cm.

Gelbsattelbarbe und Stülpmaul-Lippfisch   Yellowsaddle goatfish and Slingjaw wrasse

BARBEN GOATFISHES MULUDAE

Forsskals Barbe   Forsskal's goatfish   *Parupeneus forsskali*

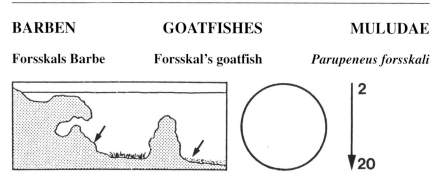

In kleinen Schwärmen sieht man die typische Rotmeerbarbe *Parupeneus forsskali* über Sandflächen ziehen. Beim Durchwühlen der oberen Schichten gesellen sich oft Lippfische dazu, die sich am aufgewirbelten Futter beteiligen.

The typical Red Sea goatfish *Parupeneus forsskali* can be seen along sandy bottoms. When they root around there in the upper layers, they are often joined by wrasses, who share in the food that is stirred up.

Großschulenbarbe   Schooling goatfish   *Mulloidichtys vanicolensis*

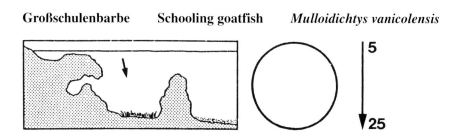

In großen Schulen bis zu 100 Fischen ist die Großschulenbarbe nicht zu übersehen. Aufgrund des schützenden Schwarmverhaltens zieht sie oft durchs freie Wasser.

Swimming in large schools of up to 100 fish, the schooling goatfish is hard to miss. On the strength of this protective schooling they often swim through open water.

Forsskals Barbe   Forsskal's goatfish   *Parupeneus forsskali*

Großschulenbarbe   Schooling goatfish   *Mulloidichtys vanicolensis*

GROSSE LIPPFISCHE   BIG WRASSES   LABRIDAE

Napoleon-Lippfisch   Napoleon wrasse   *Cheilinus undulatus*

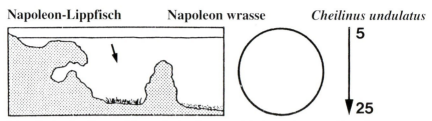

Lippfische im Roten Meer sind sehr verschiedenartig, was ihre Gestalt und Größen anbetrifft. Während des Wachstums machen sie einzigartige Farbwechsel durch, die in diesem Kapitel mit Jugend- und Altersform dokumentiert werden. Der auf dieser Seite vorgestellte Napoleon-Lippfisch kann 200 cm lang werden.

Wrasses in the Red Sea are very divergent in form and size. During their maturation they go through unique changes of colour, which are documented in this chapter by pictures of juvenile and adult variations. The Napoleon wrasse on this page can reach up to 200 cm in length.

Napoleon-Lippfisch mit Schiffshalter   Napoleon wrasse with sharksucker ▶

Napoleon-Lippfisch   Napoleon wrasse   *Cheilinus undulatus*

GROSSE LIPPFISCHE   BIG WRASSES   LABRIDAE

Rotbrustlippfisch   **Redbreasted wrasse**   *Cheilinus fasciatus*
Besenschwanzlippfisch   **Broomtail wrasse**   *Cheilinus lunulatus*
Abudjubbes Lippfisch   **Abudjubbe's wrasse**   *Cheilinus abudjubbe*

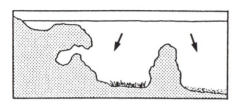 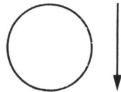

Neben dem Napoleon-Lippfisch kommen weitere attraktive Arten der Gattung *Cheilinus* im Roten Meer vor, allerdings erreichen sie seine Größe nicht.

Besides the Napoleon wrasse there are other attractive species of the genus *Cheilinus* in the Red Sea, although they do not reach the size of the former.

Abudjubbes Lippfisch   Abudjubbe's wrasse   *Cheilinus abudjubbe*

Rotbrustlippfisch   Redbreasted wrasse   *Cheilinus fasciatus*

Besenschwanzlippfisch   Broomtail wrasse   *Cheilinus lunulatus*

GROSSE LIPPFISCHE BIG WRASSES LABRIDAE

Wangenband-Lippfisch **Bandcheek wrasse** *Cheilinus digrammus*

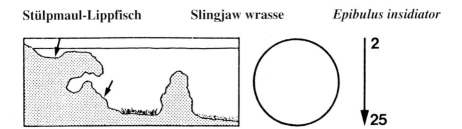

Weit verbreitet im gesamten Indopazifik ist der Wangenband-Lippfisch. Wie viele seiner Artgenossen macht er es sich mit der Futtersuche einfach und schließt sich einer Barbenschule an.

The Bandcheek Wrasse is widespread in the whole Indo-Pacific. As many others in its genus do, it simplifies its search for food by joining a school of goatfish.

Stülpmaul-Lippfisch **Slingjaw wrasse** *Epibulus insidiator*

Die ungewöhnliche Nahrungsaufnahme macht den Stülpmaul-Lippfisch auffällig. Er ist in der Lage, Krabben und Garnelen mit blitzschnellem Vorstoßen der Kiefer einzusaugen. Die Geschlechter sind deutlich unterscheidbar, hier das Weibchen, auf Seite 56 das Männchen mit der Barbe schwimmend. Ob er seine gelbe Partnerin wohl verwechselt hat?

The slingjaw wrasse has a striking way of taking in food: it can suck in crabs and shrimps with a lightning-fast extension of the jaws. The sexes are clearly distinguishable: here is the female, while on page 56 the male is pictured swimming with the goatfish. Has he perhaps mistaken it for his yellow partner?

Wangenband-Lippfisch   Bandcheek wrasse   *Cheilinus digrammus*

Stülpmaul-Lippfisch   Slingjaw wrasse   *Epibulus insidiator*

GROSSE LIPPFISCHE   BIG WRASSES   LABRIDAE

Schachbrett-Lippfisch   Checkerboard wrasse   *Halichoeres hortulanus*

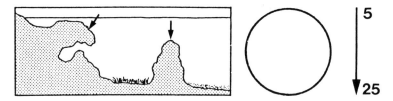

Immer in Riffnähe ist der elegant schwimmende Schachbrett-Lippfisch auf Futterdauersuche. Dabei durchstreift er ein Revier von mehreren 100 m. Die Jugendform (Insert) trägt Augenflecke zur Tarnung.

The checkerboard wrasse is always elegantly swimming close to the reef in search of food. In the course of its rounds it covers a territory several hundred metres long. The juvenile form (insert) has eye spots as deceptive coloration.

Spiegelfleck-Lippfisch   **Doublespot wrasse**   *Coris aygula*

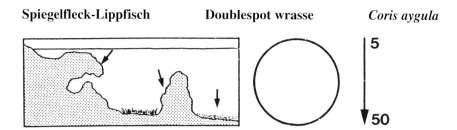

Man meint tatsächlich, zwei völlig verschiedene Fische vor sich zu haben, wenn man die Jugend-(Insert) und Altersform des Spiegelfleck-Lippfisches betrachtet. Doch man irrt, denn die orangefarbenen Flecken verblassen schnell, und es entwickelt sich daraus der grüne Riese von 100 cm.

The juvenile and adult forms of the doublespot wrasse look like two completely different fishes. But the observer would be mistaken in this conclusion, for the orange spots fade quickly as the young fish (insert) develops into the green giant of almost 100 cm.

Schachbrett-Lippfisch   Checkerboard wrasse   *Halichoeres hortulanus*

Spiegelfleck-Lippfisch   Doublespot wrasse   *Coris aygula*

KLEINE LIPPFISCHE SMALL WRASSES LABRIDAE

Zu den bekanntesten kleinen Lippfischen gehören die Putzerfische, die andere Rotmeerbewohner von Parasiten befreien. Diese Aufgabe übernehmen auch viele Jugendformen der in diesem Kapitel nicht länger als 25 cm werdenden Arten. Die Jugendform ist wieder in das Bild des erwachsenen Lippfisches eingeklinkt.

Among the best-known small wrasses are the cleaner fishes, who free the other Red Sea denizens from parasites. Many juvenile forms of the species under 25 cm in length in this chapter serve as cleaners. The respective juvenile forms are shown in insets in the pictures of the adult wrasses.

**Großzahn-Lippfisch   Bigtooth wrasse   *Macropharyngodon bipartitus*
Lyraschwanz-Lippfisch   Lyretail wrasse   *Bodianus anthioides***

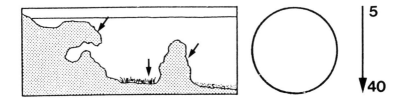

Bei fast allen Lippfischgattungen ist es so, daß sich Jungtiere (Inserts) als Weibchen entwickeln und dann ein Geschlechtswechsel zum Männchen erfolgt. Der ist auch mit einer deutlichen Veränderung des Farbkleides verbunden, wie beim Großzahn-Lippfisch und Lyraschwanz-Lippfisch erkennbar.

In almost every wrasse genus the juvenile forms (inserts) develop as females, then alter their sex to male. This also involves a significant change in coloration, as is evident with the bigtooth and lyretail wrasses.

Großzahn-Lippfisch Bigtooth wrasse *Macropharyngodon bipartitus*

Lyraschwanz-Lippfisch Lyretail wrasse *Bodianus anthioides*

KLEINE LIPPFISCHE   SMALL WRASSES   LABRIDAE

Dianas Lippfisch   Diana's wrasse   *Bodianus diana*

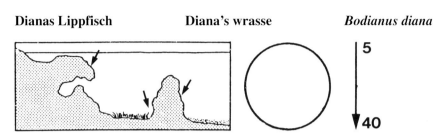

Die beiden hier vorgestellten Arten der Gattung *Bodianus* kommen nicht nur im Indopazifik, sondern auch im Roten Meer zahlreich vor. Auch Dianas Lippfisch nimmt seine Nahrung vom Boden auf und knackt mit den ausgeprägten Zähnen Schnecken und Seeigel.

These two species of the genus *Bodianus* are numerous not only in the Indo-Pacific, but also in the Red Sea. Diana's wrasse obtains its food from the sea floor, cracking open snails and sea urchins with its prominent teeth.

Mondschwanz-Lippfisch   Moontail wrasse   *Thalassoma lunare*

Lippfische graben sich mit Beginn der Dunkelheit gerne in den sandigen Untergrund ein. Dazu gehören auch die Arten der Gattung *Thalassoma*, die paarweise oder in kleinen Gruppen übers Riff ziehen. Der Mondschwanz-Lippfisch wird gerade vom indopazifischen Putzer *Labroides dimitiatus* „behandelt".

Wrasses like to bury themselves in the sandy bottom when it begins to get dark. This behaviour is also shown by the genus *Thalassoma*, which swim above the reef in pairs or small groups. The moontail wrasse in the picture is being "serviced" by the Indo-Pacific cleaner *Labroides dimitiatus*.

Dianas Lippfisch   Diana's wrasse   *Bodianus diana*

Mondschwanz-Lippfisch   Moontail wrasse   *Thalassoma lunare*

KLEINE LIPPFISCHE   SMALL WRASSES   LABRIDAE

Achtlinienlippfisch   Eightline wrasse   *Paracheilinus octotaenia*

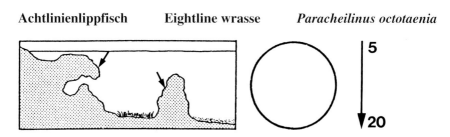

Die Schönheit von Lippfischen kommt besonders in der Balzzeit zur Geltung. Ohne Pause verfolgt hier ein Achtlinienlippfisch seit 20 Minuten eine Partnerin und zeigt ihr mit aufgestellten Flossen sein Interesse.

The beauty of the wrasses is especially apparent at courting time. The male eightline wrasse pictured here has been pursing his partner continuously for 20 minutes, and displays his interest to her with raised fins.

Rotmeerputzerlippfisch   Red sea cleaner wrasse
Larabicus quadrilineatus

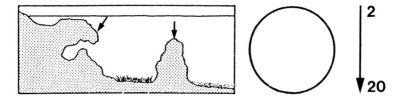

Auch im Roten Meer gibt es einen Putzerlippfisch, der nur dort vorkommt. Er verhält sich nicht anders als der indopazifische Putzerfisch und reinigt andere Riffbewohner mit seinem spitzen Mäulchen von äußeren Parasiten.

This cleaner wrasse occurs only in the Red Sea. It behaves no differently than the Indo-Pacific cleaners, cleaning ectoparasites from other reef-dwellers with his pointed snout.

Achtlinienlippfisch   Eightline wrasse   *Paracheilinus octotaenia*

Rotmeerputzerlippfisch   Red sea cleaner wrasse   *Larabicus quadrilineatus*

PAPAGEIENFISCHE   PARROTFISHES   SCARIDAE

Der populäre Name für die Familie Scaridae muß sehr schnell gefunden worden sein: Wie die gleichnamigen, farbenprächtigen Vögel haben auch Papageienfische diesen auffälligen „Schnabel" und üppige Farben. Neben den Farben fallen sie im Riff aber noch durch besondere Geräusche auf, die sie beim Abbeißen von festen Korallen erzeugen. Mit schnabelartigen Zahnplatten, die sie deutlich von den Lippfischen unterscheidet, nagen sie an Hirnkorallen, um die im Kalk wachsenden Algen aufnehmen zu können. Wenn man gelegentlich Papageienfische sieht, die eine Fahne hinter sich herziehen, so scheiden sie in diesem Moment den unverdauten Korallensand wieder aus. Papageienfische werden zum Teil 120 cm lang.

The popular name for the family Scaridae must have been found very quickly. Like the colorful birds of the same name, the parrotfishes also have the striking "beak" and sumptous colours. Besides their colours, they are also conspicuous for the special noises they make when biting off pieces of solid coral. With beaklike dental plates, which clearly distinguish them from the Labridae, they gnaw on brain corals to ingest the algae that grow in the lime. When one occasionally sees a parrotfish trailing a little cloud, this is the undigested coral sand which is being excreted. Some parrotfishes attain a length of 120 cm.

Buckelkopfpapageienfisch   Steepheaded parrotfish   *Scarus gibbus*

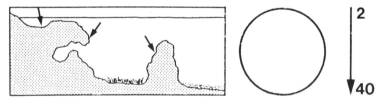

Wie bei den Lippfischen, von denen die Papageienfische abstammen, kann man Farb- und Geschlechtswechsel bei ihnen feststellen. So auch beim Buckelkopfpapageienfisch. In einer initialen Phase entwickeln sich Papageienfische als Weibchen, und in der folgenden terminalen Phase wachsen, mit dem Geschlechtswechsel zum Männchen, diese bald doppelt so groß wie die Weibchen heran.

As with the wrasses, from which the parrotfishes are descended, one also finds alterations of colour and sex. This is the case with the steepheaded parrotfish. In their initial phase parrotfishes develop as females, then mature in the following terminal phase into males, which soon grow to twice the size of the female form.

Buckelkopfpapageienfisch   Steepheaded parrotfish   *Scarus gibbus*

Scarus gibbus ♂ oben, ♀ unten

PAPAGEIENFISCHE   PARROTFISHES   SCARIDAE

Rostpapageienfisch   **Rusty parrotfish**   *Scarus ferrugineus*

Nachts schlafen Papageienfische am Boden, oft in kleinen Höhlen oder zwischen Korallen. Manche Arten entwickeln dabei eine schleimartige Hülle. Nachtaktive Garnelen suchen darauf Nahrung.

At night, parrotfishes sleep on the bottom, often in small caves or between corals. Many species secrete a veil-like sheath of muscus around themselves at this time, which nocturnal shrimps feed on.

Schlafender Rostpapageienfisch   Sleeping Rusty parrotfish

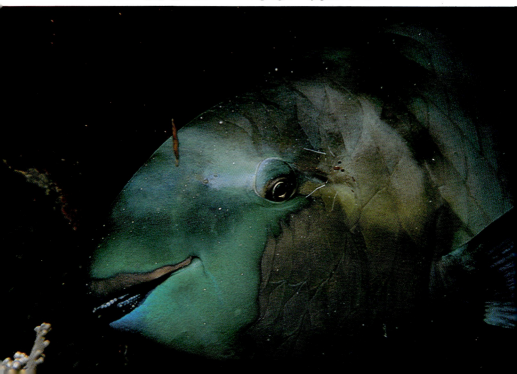

Rostpapageienfisch   Rusty parrotfish   *Scarus ferrugineus*

Scarus ferrugineus ♂ oben, ♀ unten

MURÄNEN   MORAYS   MURAENIDAE

Riesenmuräne   **Giant Moray**   *Gymnothorax javanicus*

Unverwechselbar durch ihren aalartigen Körper mit dem großen Maul sind die Muränen des Roten Meeres. Die Nachtjäger schauen tagsüber nur mit dem Kopf aus ihrer Höhle heraus. Mit etwas Glück kann der Fotograf die zum Teil über 200 cm langen Fische auch freischwimmend erleben.

Red Sea morays are unmistakable by their eel-like bodies and large mouths. The heads of these nocturnal hunters can be seen during the day peering out of their caves. With some luck a photographer can experience one of them swimming in the open. They often reach length of over 200 cm.

Riesenmuräne mit Taucherin   Giant moray with diver ▶

Riesenmuräne   Giant moray   *Gymnothorax javanicus*

MURÄNEN   MORAYS   MURAENIDAE

Schneeflockenmuräne	Snowflake moray	*Echidua nebulosa*
Graue Muräne	Grey moray	*Siderea grisea*
Rüppells Muräne	Rüppell's moray	*Gymnothorax rueppelliae*

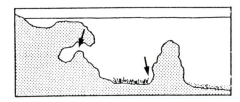 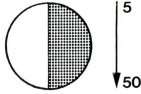

Prächtig gefärbte, aber klein bleibende Arten sind auf dieser Doppelseite abgebildet.

Small, yet magnificently coloured species are shown on these two pages.

Rüppells Muräne   Rüppell's moray   *Gymnothorax rueppelliae*

Schneeflockenmuräne   Snowflake moray   *Echidua nebulosa*

Graue Muräne   Grey moray   *Siderea grisea*

PFEIFENFISCHE

Verschiedene Familien

PIPEFISHES

Various families

Skurrile Gestalten finden wir in den Familien Syngnathidae und Solenostomidae, beide aber an der pfeifenartigen Schnauze gut als Pfeifenfische erkennbar. Obwohl nicht größer als 20 cm, ziehen die in Korallen schwimmenden Seenadeln oder die in Seegraswiesen beheimateten Seepferdchen den beobachtenden Taucher immer wieder an. Wer das Glück hat, optimale Bilder des perfekt getarnten Seegrasgeisterfisches in dessen natürlichem Lebensraum zu machen, vergißt solche Fotojagden kaum.

We find truly comical shapes in the families Syngnathidae and Solenostomidae, both readily recognizable as pipefishes by their pipelike snouts. Although not longer than 20 cm, the pipefishes swimming among the corals or the seahorses in the seagrass beds attract the observing diver over and over again. Whoever has had the good fortune to get ideal pictures of the perfectly camouflaged seagrass ghostpipefish in its natural environment will hardly forget such camera hunts.

Schultz's Seenadel   **Schultz's pipefish**   *Corythoichthys schultzi*
Schwarzbrustseenadel **Blackchest pipefish** *Corythoichthys nigripectus*

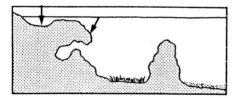 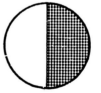

Seenadeln haben einen Körper aus knochigen Ringen. Mit der röhrenförmigen Schnauze jagen sie hauptsächlich Kleinstkrebse. Paarweise schwimmen sie in Bodennähe oder tanzen auch mal als Gruppe in einem Container eines Wracks.

Pipefishes have bodies surrounded by bony rings. With their tubelike snouts they hunt primarily tiny crustaceans. They swim in pairs near the bottom, or sometimes dance as a group in a container on a wrecked ship.

Schultz's Seenadel   Schultz's pipefish   *Corythoichthys schultzi*

Schwarzbrustseenadel   Blackchest pipefish   *Corythoichthys nigripectus*

PFEIFENFISCHE

PIPEFISHES

Blaustreifenseenadel
Dorniges Seepferdchen

Bluestripe pipefish
Thorny seahorse

Doryrhamphus excisus
Hippocampus histrix

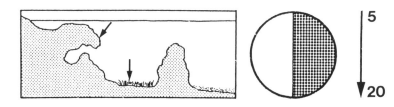

Im Gegensatz zu den Seepferdchen besitzen Seenadeln noch eine Schwanzflosse, die bei der Blaustreifennadel besonders auffällig ist. Eine biologische Einmaligkeit der Pfeifenfische ist von den Seepferdchen bekannt geworden: Der Vater gebiert die Kinder. Allerdings erst, nachdem die Mutter ihm die Eier in eine Art Bruttasche gelegt hat. Oder wie bei Seenadeln, wo sie die Eier in vorbereitete Aushöhlungen an der Körperunterseite des Seenadelmännchens plaziert. Immerhin gleicht der Geburtsvorgang beim Seepferdchen den Wehen, wenn das Männchen unter großer Anstrengung die Jungen aus der geblähten Bruttasche herauspreßt. Seepferdchen sind auch in der Hinsicht einmalig, daß sie ihren Körper vertikal bewegen, der Kopf aber horizontal auf dem Körper sitzt.

In contrast to the seahorses, the pipefishes also have a caudal fin, which is especially conspicuous on the bluestripe pipefish. The seahorses are notable for a unique biological trait of the pipefish family: the father gives birth to the young. This is, of course, after the mother has laid the eggs in a kind of pouch on his "abdomen". With the pipefish, the female lays the eggs in a concave areas prepared on the male's underside. The process of a seahorse giving birth is somewhat comparable to a woman's labor as the male presses the young out of the pouch with strenuous exertions. Seahorses are also unique in heaving the head situated horizontally on the body, although they move their bodies through the water vertically.

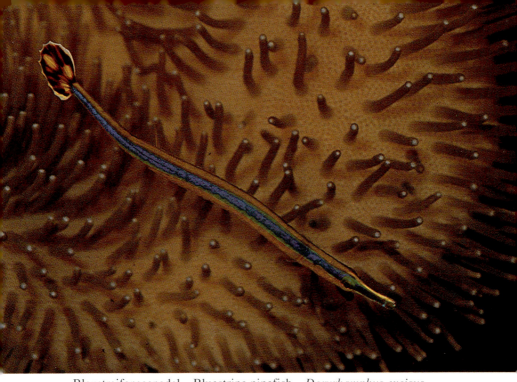

Blaustreifenseenadel   Bluestripe pipefish   *Doryrhamphus excisus*

Dorniges Seepferdchen   Thorny seahorse   *Hippocampus histrix*

PFEIFENFISCHE   PIPEFISHES

Fetzengeisterfisch   **Rag ghost pipefish**   *Solenostomus paradoxus*
Seegrasgeisterfisch   **Seagras ghost pipefish** *Solenostomus cyanopterus*

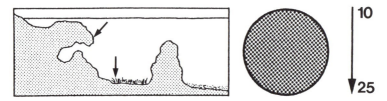

Bei den Geisterpfeifenfischen der Familie Solenostomidea ist das Geschlechtsleben normal. Sie passen sich ihrer jeweiligen Umgebung perfekt an und sind aufgrund ihrer Nachtaktivität nur sehr schwierig zu finden.

The sexual behavior of the ghostpipefishes of the family Solenostomidea is comparatively normal. They are able perfectly to adapt to their surroundings, and are very difficult to locate because of their nocturnal activity.

Fetzengeisterfisch   Rag ghost pipefish   *Solenostomus paradoxus*

Seegrasgeisterfisch in
2 Farbvarianten

Seagras ghost pipefish
with 2 colours variations

Solenostomus cyanopterus

SKORPIONSFISCHE SCORPIONFISHES SCORPAENIDAE

Kurzflossenfeuerfisch	**Shortfin turkeyfish**	*Dendrochirus brachypterus*
Strahlenfeuerfisch	**Clearfin turkeyfish**	*Pterois radiata*
Rotfeuerfisch	**Red turkeyfish**	*Pterois volitans*

2
25

Alle Skorpionsfische besitzen eine giftige Rückenflosse, die sie aber nur zur Verteidigung dem angenommenen Feind entgegenstellen. Deutlich stehen die Strahlen beim abgebildeten Rotfeuerfisch ab. Die bodengebundenen Skorpionsfische ernähren sich überfallartig von kleinen Fischen und werden 35 cm lang.

All scorpionfishes have venomous dorsal spines, which they direct only in defense against presumed enemies. The red turkeyfish pictured here displays the sharply protruding pectoral rays. The bottom-dwelling scorpionfishes, attaining a length of about 35 cm, feed primarily on small fish for which they lie in wait and then suddenly seize.

Rotfeuerfisch   Red turkeyfish   *Pterois volitans*

Kurzflossenfeuerfisch Shortfin turkeyfish *Dendrochirus brachypterus*

Strahlenfeuerfisch Clearfin turkeyfish *Pterois radiata*

SKORPIONSFISCHE SCORPIONFISHES SCORPAENIDAE

Bärtiger Drachenkopf **Bearded dragonshead** *Scorpaenopsis barbatus*
Steinfisch **Stonefish** *Synanceia verrucosa*

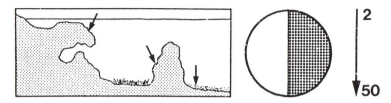

Der gefürchtetste der giftigen Fische im Roten Meer ist der Steinfisch. Wie gut er seiner Umgebung angepaßt ist, zeigt das Foto unten. Als solche verwechselt werden immer tropische Drachenköpfe. Die Kopfportraits beider Arten zeigen die Unterschiede.

The most feared of the venomous fishes in the Red Sea is the stonefish. The photo below shows how well it blends into its surroundings. They are often mistaken for tropical dragonhead fishes. The heads of both species pictured here show the differences.

Pärchen Steinfische ungeblitzt   Pair of stonefishes without flash

Bärtiger Drachenkopf   Bearded dragonshead   *Scorpaenopsis barbatus*

Steinfisch   Stonefish   *Synanceia verrucosa*

VERSCHIEDENE FISCHFAMILIEN   VARIOUS FISHFAMILIES

Von den riffbewohnenden Rotmeerfischfamilien wird lediglich eine Art in diesem Kapitel vorgestellt, deren typische Merkmale aber für die gesamte Familie zutreffen.

From each of the following reef-dwelling Red Sea fish families, only one species will be presented whose typical traits apply to its respective family as a whole.

KROKODILFISCHE   FLATHEADS   PLATYCEPHALIDAE

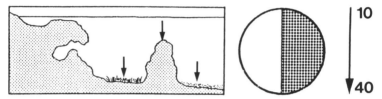

Sie liegen einzeln oder paarweise auf Sandflächen oder darin befindlichen Korallenblöcken. Im Schutze von Wracks fühlen sie sich auch wohl. Die max. 100 cm lang werdenden Krokodilfische sind Überraschungsjäger.

They lie individually or in pairs on sandy bottoms oder coral heads, and often live in the protection of wrecked ships. Reaching a maximum length of 100 cm, they specialize in surprise attacks from ambush.

FLÜGELROSSFISCHE   SEAMOTHS   PEGASIDAE

Bodengebunden leben auch die Flügelroßfische, die aber kaum länger als 20 cm werden. Tagsüber gut getarnt, sieht man sie nachts über Seegras- und Sandflächen ziehen.

The seamoths are also bottom-dwellers, but hardly exceed 20 cm. Well camouflaged by day, they can be seen at night swimming above seagrass beds and sandy bottoms.

Teppich-Krokodilfisch   Flathead   *Papilloculiceps longiceps*

Flügelroßfisch   Seamoth   *Eurypegasus draconis*

EIDECHSENFISCHE   LIZARDFISHES   SYNONTIDAE

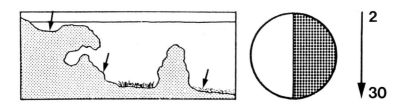

Ihren populären Namen erhielten sie wegen des reptilienartigen Kopfes. Zum Teil in den Sand eingegraben, stoßen sie blitzschnell auf vorbeischwimmende Fische und Krebse zu.

Their popular name comes from their reptile-like heads. Partly buried in the sand, they lunge with lightning speed at passing fishes and crabs.

ANGLERFISCHE   FROGFISHES   ANTENNARIIDAE

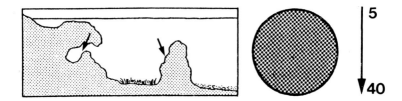

Mit dem Illicium, dem zu einer Angel umgewandelten ersten Strahl der Rückenflosse, locken Anglerfische Beute heran, die die behäbigen, aber perfekt getarnten Bodenbewohner blitzschnell in das übergroße Maul einsaugen. Das abgebildete Tier ist 3 cm lang, die Arten max. 15 cm.

With the illicium, which is its first dorsal spine transformed into a fleshly antenna, the frogfish lures its prey within range so that it can be sucked in quick as a flash by the oversized mouth. These slow and seddentary bottom-dwellers are perfectly camouflaged. The specimen pictured here is 3 cm long, though its species reaches a maximum of 15 cm.

Eidechsenfisch Lizardfish *Synodus variegatus*

Anglerfisch Frogfish *Antennarius coccineus*

FLÖTENFISCHE CORNETFISHES FISTULARIIDAE

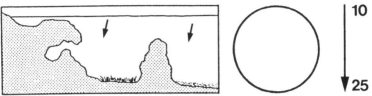

Häufig und gleich gruppenweise trifft man im Roten Meer die Flötenfische an, sie sind mit den bekannteren Trompetenfischen verwandt. Das scheinbar kleine Maul der 150 cm langen Fische kann durchaus Riffbarsche aufnehmen.

In the Red Sea one encounters the cornetfishes frequently in groups. They are related to the better-known trumpetfishes. The apparently small mouth of the 150 cm fish is quite capable of swallowing damselfish.

WELSE EEL CATFISHES PLOTOSIDAE

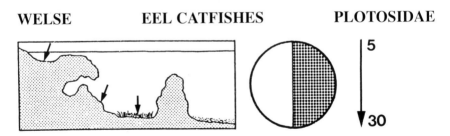

Welse ziehen schwarmweise an den Riffen des Roten Meeres entlang. Sie sind deutlich an den Barteln ums Maul zu erkennen. Die Rückenflosse der max. 30 cm langen Fische ist giftig!

Eel catfishes swim in schools along the reefs of the Red Sea, and are easily recognizable by the barbels around the mouth. Reaching a maximum of 30 cm, these fishes have a venomous dorsal fin!

Flötenfisch   Cornetfish   *Fistularia commersonii*

Gestreifter Wels   Striped eel catfish   *Plotosus lineatus*

FLEDERMAUSFISCHE   BATFISHES   EPHIPPIDAE

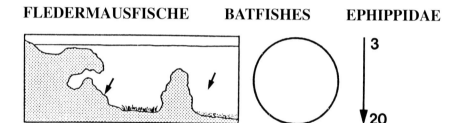

Seltener als im Indopazifik sieht man im Roten Meer die großen Schwärme von Fledermausfischen. Die beinahe runden, hochgebauten Körper stehen dann wie eine Wand im freien Wasser vor Dropoffs. Die bis zu 40 cm langen Altfische ziehen sich auch einzeln ins Riff zurück.

The large schools of batfishes are seen in the Red Sea less often than in the Indo-Pacific. The nearly round, deep body stands like a wall in the open water in front of dropoffs. The adults, reaching a length of 40 cm, also live als solitaries in the reef.

FEILENFISCHE   FILEFISHES   MONACANTHIDAE

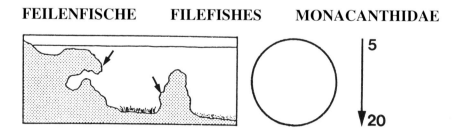

Die den Drückerfischen ähnlich sehenden Feilenfische unterscheiden sich von diesen durch den noch mehr komprimierten Körper, der längeren Schnauze und nur einem langen Rückenflossenstrahl. Lediglich die hier abgebildete Art wird 40 cm lang, sonst erreichen sie max. 20 cm.

The filefishes are distinguished from the similar triggerfishes by the more compressed body, the longer snout, and the single, long dorsal spine. Only the species shown here reaches 40 cm; others grow to a maximum of only 20 cm.

Schwarmfledermausfisch   Schooling batfish   *Platax orbicularis*

Besenschwanzfeilenfisch   Broomtail filefish   *Aluterus scriptus*

KOFFERFISCHE BOXFISHES OSTRACIIDAE

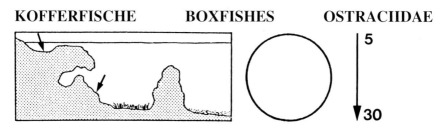

Ihr harter und rechteckiger Körper hat dieser Familie ihren Namen gegeben. Kofferfische propellern etwas unbeholfen mit den Rücken- und Analflossen umher und nutzen nur die Schwanzflosse zum Beschleunigen. Mit dem spitzen Mäulchen suchen sie am Boden lebende Niedere Tiere. Sie werden 45 cm lang.

This family has its name from the hard, angular bodies of its members. Boxfishes propel themselves somewhat awkwardly with their dorsal and anal fins, and only use the tail fin for speed. With their pointed mouths, they search along the bottom for invertebrates to feed on, and reach a length of 45 cm.

BLITZLICHTFISCHE FLASHLIGHTFISHES
ANOMALOPIDAE

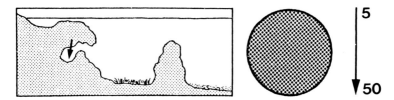

Ihre Verwandten sind nur in Tauchern unzugängigen Tiefen zu finden, aber der abgebildete Blitzlichtfisch kommt im Roten Meer schon in wenigen Metern Tiefe vor. Unter jedem Auge tragen sie ein leuchtendes Organ, das sie ein- und ausschalten können. Sie benutzen es zur Kommunikation untereinander und um Feinde zu verwirren. Max. Länge 11 cm.

Their relatives occur only in depths inaccessible to divers, but the flashlight fish pictured here lives at depth of only a few metres in the Red Sea. Below each eye is a luminescent organ which it can switch off and on. They use this to communicate with one another and to confuse predators. They reach a maximum length of only 11 cm.

Gelber Kofferfisch   Yellow boxfish   *Ostracion cubicus*

Rotmeerblitzfisch   Red sea flashlightfish   *Photoblepharon steinitzi*

STACHELMAKRELEN   JACKS   CARANGIDAE

Torpedomakrele   **Torpedo jack**   *Scomberoides Iysan*
Großaugenmakrele   **Bigeye jack**   *Caranx sexfasciatus*

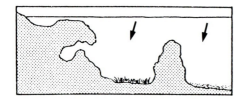 

Die schnellschwimmenden, silberfarbenen Fische sind Riffbesucher aus dem offenen Meer. Die große, gegabelte Schwanzflosse treibt den Hochgeschwindigkeitskörper dabei an. Sie werden 150 cm lang.

These fast swimming, silvery fishes are reef visitors from the open sea. The large forked tail fin propels the highly streamlined body. Jacks reach a length of 150 cm.

Torpedomakrele   Torpedo jack   *Scomberoides Iysan*

Großaugenmakrele   Bigeye jack   *Caranx sexfasciatus*

Balzendes Paar Großaugenmakrele   Courting pair of Bigeye jacks

STACHELMAKRELEN   JACKS   CARANGIDAE

Orangenfleckmakrele   **Orangespotted jack**   *Carangoides bajad*
Blauflossenmakrele   **Bluefin jack**   *Caranx melampygus*
Dickkopfmakrele   **Bighead jack**   *Caranx ignobilis*

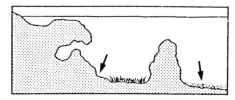

Makrelen im Roten Meer sind Herdenfische bis zu mehreren Hundert. Durch geschicktes Jagen kesseln sie Jungfischschwärme ein, um sie zu erbeuten.

Jacks in the Red Sea travel in schools of up to several hundred. By skillful hunting they surround schools of young fish in order to capture them.

Orangenfleckmakrele   Orangespotted jack   *Carangoides bajad*

Blauflossenmakrele Bluefin jack *Caranx melampygus*

Dickkopfmakrele Bighead jack *Caranx ignobilis*

BARRAKUDAS   BARRACUDAS   SPHYRAENIDAE

Großschulenbarrakuda	**Schooling barracuda**	*Sphyraena quenie*
Großer Barrakuda	**Great barracuda**	*Sphyraena barracuda*
Silberstrich-Barrakuda	**Chevron barracuda**	*Sphyraena jello*

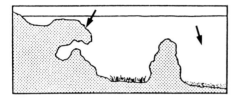 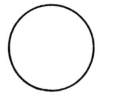

3
40

Die Furcht vor Barrakudas ist übertrieben: Auch große Einzelgänger attackieren nicht grundlos einen Taucher, es sei denn, er transportiert blutende Fische. Normalerweise jagen die zylindrisch geformten Räuber schwarmweise im freien Wasser.

The fear of barracudas is exaggerated. Even large, solitary specimens do not attack a diver without reason, as when the diver is carrying bleeding fishes, for example. The cylindrically-shaped predators usually hunt in schools in the open water.

Großschulenbarrakuda   Schooling barracuda   *Sphyraena quenie*

Großer Barrakuda   Great barracuda   *Sphyraena barracuda*

Silberstrich-Barrakuda   Chevron barracuda   *Sphyraena jello*

SCHNAPPER / SNAPPERS

Verschiedene Familien / **Various families**

Schwarzweißschnapper — Black and white snapper — *Macolor niger*
Einfleckschnapper — Onespot snapper — *Lutjanus monostigma*
Zweifleckschnapper — Twinspot snapper — *Lutjanus bohar*

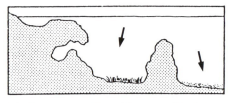 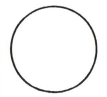

Die kommerziell wichtigsten Fischfamilien sind in diesem Kapitel zusammengefaßt. Sie ernähren sich von Krebsen und anderen Fischen und formieren sich in Riffnähe oft zu Schulen. Ausgewachsene Einzelgänger werden 100 cm lang.

The fish families most important commercially are placed together in this chapter. They feed on crabs and other fish, and often form schools near the reefs. Fully grown solitaries reach 100 cm.

Schwarzweißschnapper   Black and white snapper   *Macolor niger*

Einfleckschnapper   Onespot snapper   *Lutjanus monostigma*

Zweifleckschnapper   Twinspot snapper   *Lutjanus bohar*

SCHNAPPER   SNAPPER

Verschiedene Familien

Blauschuppenschnapper   Bluescale snapper   *Lethrinus nebulosus*
Schwarzgep. Süßlippe   Blackspotted sweetlip   *Plectorhynchus gaterinus*
Großaugenschnapper   Bigeye snapper   *Monotaxis grandoculis*

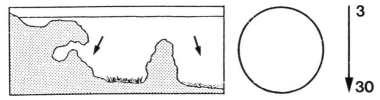

Wenn ich die Familien Haemulidae und Lethrinidae populär weiter als Schnapper bezeichne, so deshalb, weil sie eng mit den Lutjanidae verwandt sind. Ihr Verhalten im Riff ist ebenfalls ähnlich.

When I populary designate the families Haemulidae and Lethrinidae as snappers, it is because they are related to the Lutjanidae. Their behavior in the reef is likewise similar.

Blauschuppenschnapper   Bluescale snapper   *Lethrinus nebulosus*

Schwarzgepunktete Süßlippe   Blackspotted sweetlip   *Plectorhynchus gaterinus*

Großaugenschnapper   Bigeye snapper   *Monotaxis grandoculis*

BRASSEN BREAMS SPARIDAE

Zweibandbrasse   Doublebar bream   *Acanthopagrus bifasciatus*

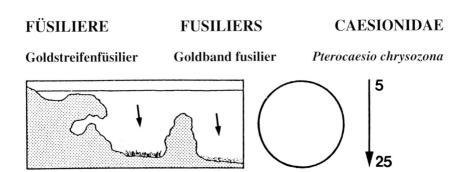

Unter den Brassen gibt es im Unterschied zu den Schnappern auch Arten, die pflanzliche Kost zu sich nehmen. Die Zweibandbrasse schwimmt normalerweise im Schwarm, nur Alttiere sondern sich ab. Sie werden 50 cm lang.

In contrast to the snappers, there are species of breams that feed on plants as well. The doublebar bream normally swims in schools. Only older specimens split off the school. They grow to 50 cm.

FÜSILIERE FUSILIERS CAESIONIDAE

Goldstreifenfüsilier   Goldband fusilier   *Pterocaesio chrysozona*

Wesentlich schlanker als Schnapper ziehen sie in riesigen Schwärmen durch das freie Wasser im Roten Meer, immer auf Jagd nach Plankton. Ihre farblich attraktivste Art von 18 cm Länge ist der Goldstreifenfüsilier.

Considerably slimmer than snappers, fusiliers swim in huge schools through the open waters of the Red Sea, always in search of plankton. The most colourful species, 18 cm long, is the goldband fusilier.

Zweibandbrasse   Doublebar bream   *Acanthopagrus bifasciatus*

Goldstreifenfüsilier   Goldband fusilier   *Pterocaesio chrysozona*

DRÜCKERFISCHE   TRIGGERFISHES   BALISTIDAE

Gelbschwanzdrücker   Yellowtail trigger   *Balistapus undulatus*

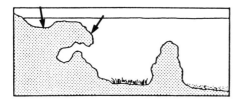 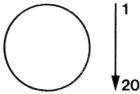

Unverwechselbar sind die Arten der Familie Balistidae aufgrund ihrer eigenwilligen Körperform, wobei der Kopf allein ein Drittel des Körpers einnimmt. Die Einzelgänger knacken mit ihren scharfen und wuchtigen Zähnen Krebse, Seeigel oder auch Steinkorallen. Bei Gefahr verankern sie sich in ihren kleinen Höhlen mit dem ersten der drei verlängerten Rückenflossenstrahlen. Ein hartes Bauchflossenrudiment, das sie ebenfalls starr aufrichten können, gibt auf der anderen Körperseite den Halt. Als Taucher kann man die Verankerung lösen, indem man wie bei einem Gewehr auf den zweiten Rückenflossenstrahl drückt, womit die Sperre aufgehoben wird. Der furchtsame Drücker wird sich das aber mit einem lauten „tok – tok – tok!" verbieten. Die größte Drückerfischart wird 70 cm lang.

The species of the Family Balistidae are unmistakeable in their peculiar body shape, whereby the head alone makes up a third of the fish's length. The solitaries crack crabs, sea urchins, or even stone corals with their sharp and powerful teeth. When threatened, they anchor themselves in their holes with the first of the three extended dorsal spines. A hard, rudimentary pelvic fin that can likewise be rigidly erected holds the lower part of the body fast. As a diver one can loosen the hold by pressing on the second dorsal spine as on a trigger, which releases the blocking action. The frightened triggerfish will protest this with a loud "tok – tok – tok!" The largest triggerfish species grow to 70 cm.

Gelbschwanzdrücker   Yellowtail trigger   *Balistapus undulatus*

DRÜCKERFISCHE TRIGGERFISHES BALISTIDAE

Riesendrücker **Titan trigger** *Balistoides viridescens*

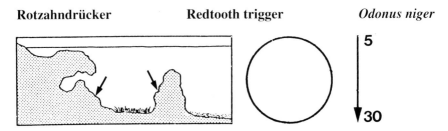

Für den Taucher ist der Riesendrückerfisch der gefährlichste Fisch, der ihm überhaupt unter Wasser begegnen kann. Insbesondere wenn er in einer Sandmulde sein Gelege bewacht, ist es nicht ratsam, dicht vorbeizuschwimmen. Ausgestanzte Löcher in den Flossen und Fleischwunden an den Armen einiger Taucher zeugen von der Aggressivität des mit mächtigen Hauern versehenen Riesendrückers, der bis zu 70 cm lang wird.

For a diver the titan triggerfish is the most dangerous fish he can encounter underwater. Especially when it is guarding its egg mass in a sandy trough, it is advisable not to swim close by. Divers with flesh wounds and holes in their fins testify to the agressiveness of the titan triggerfish and its powerful teeth. They grow to a length of 70 cm.

Rotzahndrücker **Redtooth trigger** *Odonus niger*

Der Rotzahndrücker ist geradezu das Gegenteil. Diese Art steht manchmal in kleinen Schulen im freien Wasser, schießt aber sofort in die bodennahen Verstecke, wenn ein Taucher naht. Meist schaut dann lediglich die Schwanzflosse aus dem Riff heraus.

The redtooth triggerfish is just the opposite. This species will sometimes hang in the open water in small schools, but dart immediately into concealment near the bottom when a divers near. All one sees then is the tail fin protuding from the reef.

Riesendrücker   Titan trigger   *Balistoides viridescens*

Rotzahndrücker   Redtooth trigger   *Odonus niger*

DRÜCKERFISCHE   TRIGGERFISHES   BALISTIDAE

Blauer Drücker   **Blue trigger**   *Pseudobalistes fuscus*
Rotmeerpicassodrücker   **Red sea picasso trigger**   *Rhinecanthus assasi*
Weißschwanzflossendrücker   **Whitetail trigger**   *Sufflamen albicaudatus*

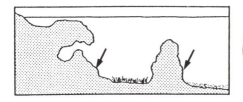 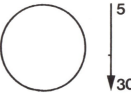

Im Roten Meer kommen zwei Arten vor, die es nur dort gibt. Sie sind rechts abgebildet. Für manche Drücker-Einzelgänger sind Wracks eine willkommene Behausung.

Two species which occur exclusively in the Red Sea are pictured on the right. Wrecks are a welcome shelter for solitary triggers.

Blauer Drücker   **Blue trigger**   *Pseudobalistes fuscus*

Rotmeerpicassodrücker   Red sea picasso trigger   *Rhinecanthus assasi*

Weißschwanzflossendrücker   Whitetail trigger   *Sufflamen albicaudatus*

KUGELFISCHE PUFFERS TETRAODONTIDAE

Kronenkugelfisch Crownpuffer *Canthigaster coronata*
Zwergkugelfisch Dwarfpuffer *Canthigaster pygmaea*

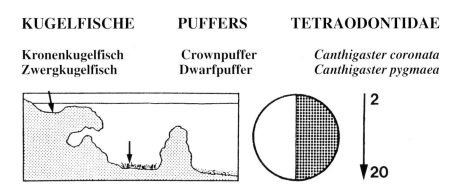

Ob kleinbleibende Arten wie die der Unterfamilie Canthigasterinae oder die bis 90 cm werdenden Arten der Tetraodontinae: Alle besitzen die Fähigkeit, ihren Körper kugelartig mit Wasser aufzupumpen, vor allem um den angenommenen Freßfeind – oft ist es ein neugieriger Taucher – von seinem Vorhaben abzuschrecken. Vom Verzehr eines Kugelfisches ist grundsätzlich abzuraten, denn deren giftige Innereien können zum Tod führen. Mit dem kräftigen, aus Zahnplatten bestehenden Gebiß verspeisen Kugelfische mit Vorliebe Krebstiere. Mit etwas Glück kann man diese einzelgängerisch lebenden Fische während der Balz auch in kleinen Schulen antreffen. Die kleinen *Canthigaster*-Arten im Roten Meer passen auch noch aufgepumpt in die Handfläche eines Tauchers. Tagsüber sind sie sehr scheu, nachts jedoch kann man sie eher mit der Kamera festhalten.

Whether it is the small species, as in the subfamily Canthigasterinae, or the up to 90 cm long species of the Tetraodontinae, all have the ability to pump up their bodies with water into a round shape, primarily to discourage a presumed predator – often it is a curious diver. It is quite inadvisable to eat puffers, for toxic organs can lead to death if consumed. Using strong jaws equipped with hard dental plates, puffers prefer to dine on crustaceans. With luck, one can encounter schools of these usually solitary fish during courting time. The little *Canthigaster* species in the Red Sea fit into a diver's hand even when puffed up. During the day they are very shy, and one can more readily catch them with a camera at night.

Kronenkugelfisch   Crownpuffer   *Canthigaster coronata*

Zwergkugelfisch   Dwarfpuffer   *Canthigaster pygmaea*

KUGELFISCHE   PUFFERS   TETRAODONTIDAE

Weißfleckkugelfisch   **Whitespotted puffer**   *Arothron hispidus*
Maskenkugelfisch   **Masked puffer**   *Arothron diadematus*

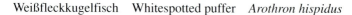

Zwar immer in Bodennähe, schwimmen die größeren Kugelfischarten aber auch tagsüber frei vor dem Riff.

Although always close to the bottom, the larger puffer species also swim in the open in front of the reef during the day.

Weißfleckkugelfisch   Whitespotted puffer   *Arothron hispidus*

Maskenkugelfisch vor Rotmeerriff   Mask Puffer in front of a Red Sea reef

Maskenkugelfisch   Masked puffer   *Arothron diadematus*

KUGELFISCHE   PUFFERS   TETRAONDONTIDAE

Schwarzfleckkugelfisch   Blackspotted puffer   *Arothron stellatus*

|5

|40

Der größte im Roten Meer schwimmende Kugelfisch trägt deutlich sichtbare schwarze Flecken auf weißem Untergrund. Wie alle Artgenossen bewegt er sich auf der Suche nach Krebsen mit der Rücken- und Afterflosse.

The largest of the Red Sea puffers has distinct black spots on a white background. As all others in its family, it propels itself with its dorsal and anal fins as it searches for crabs.

Rotmeerigelfisch   Red sea burrfish   *Chilomycterus spilostylus*

|5

|30

Eng mit den Kugelfischen verwandt, unterscheiden sich die Igelfische durch mehr oder weniger lange Stacheln am gesamten Körper. Die Schwimmweise und das Nahrungsverhalten ist gleich dem der Kugelfische.

Closely related to the puffers, the burrfishes are distinguished by the shorter or longer spines over the whole body. They swim and feed the same as the puffers.

Schwarzfleckkugelfisch   Blackspotted puffer   *Arothron stellatus*

Rotmeerigelfisch   Red sea burrfish   *Chilomycterus spilostylus*

SOLDATENFISCHE
Verschiedene Familien

Riesenhusar

SOLDIERFISHES
Various families

Giant squirrelfish *Sargocentron spinifer*

 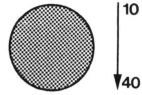

Recht unterschiedliche Fischfamilien faßt man populär als Soldatenfische zusammen. Alle Arten haben aber gemeinsam, daß sie überwiegend rot gefärbt sind und große Augen besitzen. Das läßt auf versteckte Lebensweise und Nachtaktivität schließen. Trotzdem sieht man sie tagsüber im hinteren Bereich von Höhlen und Überhängen. Einige Arten als kleine Schulen, die großgewachsenen, wie rechts abgebildet, als Einzelgänger. Nach Öffnung des Suezkanals sind einige Rotmeersoldatenfische auch in das Mittelmeer eingewandert. Der größte Soldatenfisch ist jedem Rotmeertaucher bekannt. Er wird 45 cm lang und ernährt sich von Krebstieren und kleineren Fischen.

Some quite different fish families are populary grouped together as soldierfishes. All these species, however, have large eyes and mostly reddish coloration in common. These characteristics point to secretive behavior and nocturnal activity. In spite of this, one does see them during the day in the backs of caves and overhangs. Some species live in small schools, then become solitary when fully grown, as the ones pictured here. After the Suez Canal was opened, some squirrelfishes migrated into the Mediterranean.
The largest soldierfish is familiar to Red Sea divers. It grows to 45 cm and feeds on crustaceans and smaller fishes.

Riesenhusar   Giant squirrelfish   *Sargocentron spinifer*

SOLDATENFISCHE SOLDIERFISHES

Großaugenbarsch **Bigeye** *Priacanthus hamrur*

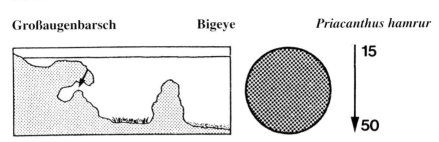

Besonders groß sind die Augen dieser Fischfamilie *Priacanthidae*. Vom Großaugenbarsch weiß man, daß er nachts die Färbung ändert, er wirkt dann silbrig.

The bigeye family *Priacanthidae* has especially large eyes. It is known that bigeyes change their colour at night, when they appear silvery.

Blutfleck-Husar **Torpedo squirrelfish** *Neoniphon sammara*

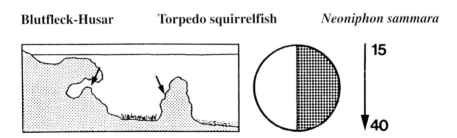

Tagsüber nicht so versteckt wie andere Soldatenfische lebt der Blutfleck-Husar im Roten Meer. Man trifft ihn sogar an festen Putzerstationen im Riff an.

The torpedo squirrelfish is not as secretive during the day as the other soldierfishes, and can be encontered at fixed cleaning stations in the reef.

Großaugenbarsch   Bigeye   *Priacanthus hamrur*

Blutfleck-Husar   Torpedo squirrelfish   *Neoniphon sammara*

KAISERFISCHE ANGELFISHES POMACANTHIDAE

Imperatorkaiserfisch	Emperor angelfish	*Pomacanthus imperator*
Arabischer Kaiserfisch	Arabian angelfish	*Pomacanthus maculosus*

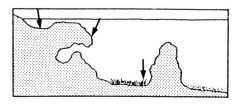 

Mit den Falterfischen haben sie vieles gemeinsam, bilden dennoch die eigene Familie Pomacanthidae. Deutlich unterscheidet man Kaiserfische an einem Dorn am unteren Kiemendeckel. Die Färbungen variieren von Art zu Art ganz erheblich, insbesondere sind manchmal die Jugendformen anders gefärbt als die Alttiere (Inserts). Beispiele davon sind eingeklinkt. Kaiserfische ernähren sich von Schwämmen und Algen, aber auch von Zooplankton aus dem freien Wasser. Die größte Rotmeerart wird 50 cm lang. Wie unterschiedlich Jugend- und Altersform sind, zeigen der Imperatorkaiser und der Arabische Kaiser. Der erste ist bis in den Pazifik, der zweite um die Arabische Halbinsel bis in den Persischen Golf verbreitet. Beide sind im gesamten Roten Meer recht häufig.

These have much in common with the butterflyfishes, yet constitute their own family of Pomacanthidae. An angelfish is distinguishable as such by the spine on the lower operculum. The coloration varies considerably from species to species, and the juvenile color patterns are sometimes quite different from those of the adult stage (inserts). Examples are in the photo insets. They feed on sponges and algae, but also on zooplankton in the open water. The largest Red Sea species reaches 50 cm. The Emperor and Arabian angelfishes are examples of how different the juvenile and adult colors can be. The former occurs out into the Pacific, the latter around the Arabian Peninsula into the Arabian Gulf. Both are quite common everywhere in the Red Sea.

Imperatorkaiserfisch   Emperor angelfish   *Pomacanthus imperator*

Arabischer Kaiserfisch   Arabian angelfish   *Pomacanthus maculosus*

KAISERFISCHE   ANGELFISHES   POMACANTHIDAE

Halbmondkaiserfisch   **Crescent angelfish**   *Pomacanthus asfur*

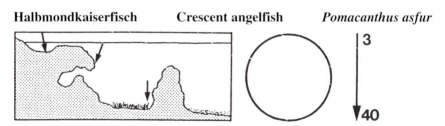

Für mich ist der Halbmondkaiserfisch der schönste im Roten Meer. Wie intensiv seine Sichel im Vergleich zum Arabischen Kaiserfisch ist, zeigt ein Schnappschuß aus trüben saudiarabischen Gewässern, wo beide zusammen schwimmen. Der Halbmondkaiserfisch bleibt kleiner als der Arabische Kaiserfisch.

To me, the crescent angelfish is the most beautiful in the Red Sea. The intensity of its sickle compared to that of the Arabian angelfish is shown in this photo taken in murky Saudi Arabian waters, where both are swimming together. The crescent angelfish remains smaller than the Arabian angelfish.

Verwechslung ausgeschlossen: *Pomacanthus asfur* und *Pomacanthus maculosus*

A mix-up between these two is out of conclusion: *P. asfur* and *P. maculosus*

Halbmondkaiserfisch   Crescent angelfish   *Pomacanthus asfur*

Halbmondkaiserfisch zupft an Schwamm   Crescent angel feeds on sponge

KAISERFISCHE   ANGELFISHES   POMACANTHIDAE

Pfauenkaiserfisch   **Royal angelfish**   *Pygoplites diacanthus*

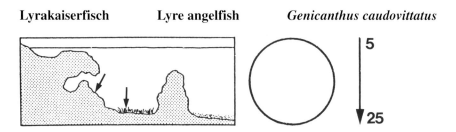

Natürlich ist der Pfauenkaiserfisch ein Wunder an Farbenpracht, sogar im Jugendstadium (Insert). Die einzige Art seiner Gattung ist im Roten Meer und im Indopazifik weit verbreitet.

The royal angelfish is a marvel of colorful splendour, even in the juvenile stage (insert). The only species in its genus, it is widespread in the Red Sea and the Indo-Pacific.

Lyrakaiserfisch   **Lyre angelfish**   *Genicanthus caudovittatus*

Während ausgewachsene Männchen und Weibchen der Rotmeerkaiserfische dasselbe Kleid tragen, gilt das nicht für den Lyrakaiserfisch. Die abgebildete Balzszene zeigt im Vordergrund das gestreifte Männchen, das mit aufgestellten Flossen erregt das graue Weibchen anbalzt.

While fully grown males and females of the Red Sea angelfishes generally look the same, this is not true of the lyre angelfish. The courting scene pictured here shows in the foreground the striped male in arousal as he approaches the gray female with his fins raised.

Pfauenkaiserfisch   Royal angelfish   *Pygoplites diacanthus*

Lyrakaiserfisch   Lyre angelfish   *Genicanthus caudovittatus*

KAISERFISCHE   ANGELFISHES   POMACANTHIDAE

Rotmeerrauchkaiser   Red sea smoke angelfish   *Apolemichthys xanthotis*

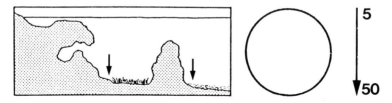

Recht selten sieht der Taucher den Rotmeerrauchkaiser, eher noch an der Ostküste als an der Westküste, wo er nur sehr tief vorkommt (unter 50 m). Über dem Kiemendeckel trägt er einen gelben Fleck.

Divers seldom catch a glimpse of this angelfish, but when they do, it is more readily on the east coast than on the west coast, where it only occurs at greater depth below 50 m. It bears a yellow spot above the upper end of the gill opening.

Rotmeerzwergkaiser   Red sea dwarfangelfish   *Centropyge multispinis*

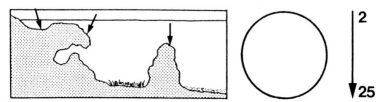

Nicht sehr attraktiv, aber zweifellos der häufigste Kaiserfisch im Roten Meer ist der Rotmeerzwergkaiserfisch als einziger seiner Gattung. Der wendige Winzling schaut aus fast jedem Korallenstock heraus, verschwindet aber im selben Moment wieder darin.

The only member of its genus, this angelfish is not so attractive, but is doubtlessly the most numerous angelfish in the Red Sea. The agile little fellow is seen peeking out of nearly every coral, but disappears back into it in the same moment.

Rotmeerrauchkaiser   Red sea smoke angelfish   *Apolemichthys xanthotis*

Rotmeerzwergkaiser   Red sea dwarfangelfish   *Centropyge multispinis*

FALTERFISCHE BUTTERFLYFISHES
CHAETODONTIDAE

Obwohl sie wie die Kaiserfische normalerweise einzeln oder paarweise schwimmen, gibt es bei den zur Familie Chaetodontidae gehörenden Falter- und Wimpelfischen im Roten Meer einige Ausnahmen, die sicherlich tauchende Fotografen und Filmer erfreuen: Wenn farbintensive Falterschulen vorbeischwimmen, zwingen sie zum Auslösen der Kamera! Die Hälfte der hier vorkommenden Falter- und Wimpelfische gibt es nur im Roten Meer. Die tagaktiven, beweglichen Schwimmer ernähren sich von Korallenpolypen oder frei treibendem Zooplankton. Nur eine Art, dier Riesenfalterfisch, wird länger als 20 cm.

Although they normally swim single or in pairs like the angelfish, there are some exeptions among butterflyfishes and bannerfishes of the family Chaetodontidae in the Red Sea. When such colorful butterflyfish schools swim past, they almost force the delighted photographers and cameramen to take a picture! Half of the butterflyfishes and bannerfishes found here occur only in the Red Sea. These diurnal mobile swimmers feed on coral polyps or drifting zooplankton. Only one species, the giant, or lined butterflyfish, exceeds 20 cm.

Maskenfalterfisch   **Masked butterflyfish**   *Chaetodon semilarvatus*

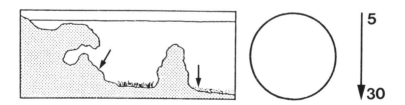

Maskenfalterfische sind typische Rotmeerbewohner und fallen im sonnendurchfluteten Riff besonders auf.

Masked butterflyfishes are typical Red Sea inhabitants, and are expecially conspicuous in sunlit reefs.

Maskenfalterfisch   Masked butterflyfish   *Chaetodon semilarvatus*

Diese Art schwimmt gern in Schulen   This species prefers to swim in schools

FALTERFISCHE BUTTERFLYFISHES
CHAETODONTIDAE

Tabakfalterfisch   Racoon butterflyfish   *Chaetodon fasciatus*

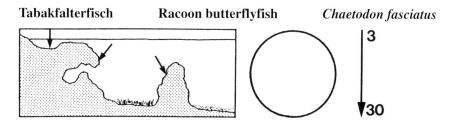

Wie viele andere Rotmeerbewohner hat auch der Tabakfalter das Bedürfnis, sich von äußeren Parasiten reinigen zu lassen. Diese Dienste bestreiten nicht nur die bereits erwähnten Putzerlippfische, sondern auch verschiedene Garnelen. Hier sucht das Pärchen Tabakfalter den Standort der Garnelen auf und gibt durch für beide Partner verständliche Signale zu verstehen, daß es geputzt werden möchte. Sofort springen die Putzergarnelen *Lysmata amboinensis* auf den Körper der Fische und hebeln die zum Teil für sie schmackhaften Parasiten ab. Wo findet man die in diesem Buch oft gezeigten Jugendformen der Fische, insbesondere die der Falterfische? Sie sind nur max. 2 cm lang und schon aus diesem Grund nicht auffällig. Ich konnte sie nicht in großen Tiefen, sondern auf den mit Korallen übersäten Flachriffen, manchmal direkt unter der Wasseroberfläche fotografieren.

As many other Red Sea dwellers, the racoon butterflyfish also needs to be cleaned of ectoparasites. Not only the cleaner wrasses take care of this service, but also various shrimps' location and have given the signals, understandable for both sides, that they want to be cleaned. The cleaner shrimps *(Lysmata amboinensis)* immediately jump up to the fish's bodies and lift off the parasites, some of which they find very palatable. Where does one find the juvenile forms of the fishes often pictured in this book – especially the butterflyfishes? They are only 2 cm long at the most, and for this reason alone inconspicuous. I wasn't able to photograph them in greater depth, but rather on the reefflats covered with corals, sometimes directly under the surface of the water.

Tabakfalterfisch   Racoon butterflyfish   *Chaetodon fasciatus*

Tabakfalterfisch in typischer Umgebung   Racoon butterfly in typical habitat

FALTERFISCHE BUTTERFLYFISHES
CHAETODONTIDAE

Rotfleckfalterfisch   Redback butterflyfish   *Chaetodon paucifasciatus*

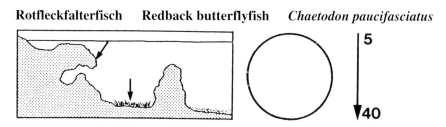

Normalerweise schwimmt der Rotfleckfalterfisch paarweise, manchmal auch in kleinen Gruppen. Er sucht sein Futter auch in Seegraswiesen.

The redback butterflyfish normally swim in pairs, sometimes also in small groups. They find their food in seagrass beds.

Polypenfalterfisch   Polyp butterflyfish   *Chaetodon austriacus*

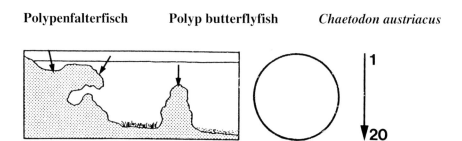

Ein Nahrungsspezialist ist der Polypenfalterfisch, denn er ernährt sich ausschließlich von Korallenpolypen. Seine Jungtiere verstecken sich immer in den Verästelungen von Steinkorallen.

This species has a specialized diet, feeding exclusively on coral polyps. Its young always hide in the branches of the stone corals.

Rotfleckfalterfisch   Redback butterflyfish   *Chaetodon paucifasciatus*

Polypenfalterfisch   Polyp butterflyfish   *Chaetodon austriacus*

FALTERFISCHE   BUTTERFLYFISHES
CHAETODONTIDAE

Fähnchenfalterfisch   **Threadfin butterflyfish**   *Chaetodon auriga*

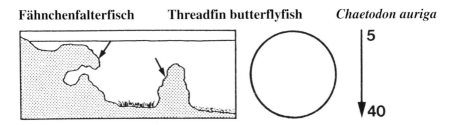

Das typische Merkmal des Fähnchenfalters ist das Filament am Ende der Rückenflosse, das sonst kein anderer Rotmeerfalterfisch trägt. Schwimmt einzeln oder paarweise.

The typical trait of the threadfin butterflyfish ist the filament at the end of the dorsal fin, not found otherwise on any of the other Red Sea butterflyfishes. It swims alone or in pairs.

Orangenkopffalterfisch   **Orangeface butterflyfish**   *Chaetodon larvatus*

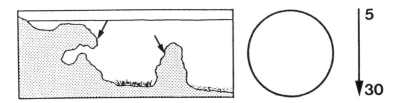

Während alle anderen Rotmeerfalter im gesamten Bereich vorkommen, ist der Orangenfalterfisch im Norden des Roten Meeres nicht verbreitet. Auch er zupft mit Vorliebe an Korallenpolypen.

While all the other Red Sea butterflyfishes are found throughout the sea, the orangeface butterflyfish does not range into the northern part. It also prefers to pluck at coral polyps.

Fähnchenfalterfisch   Threadfin butterflyfish   *Chaetodon auriga*

Orangenkopffalterfisch   Orangeface butterflyfish   *Chaetodon larvatus*

FALTERFISCHE   BUTTERFLYFISHES
CHAETODONTIDAE

Gelbsaumfalterfisch   Yellowedge butterflyfish   *Chaetodon melannotus*

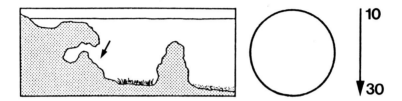

Beim genauen Betrachten fällt dem Beobachter von Falterfischen im Roten Meer sicherlich auf, daß viele Arten eine „Augenbinde" tragen, so auch der Gelbsaumfalterfisch. Darunter versteckt liegt immer das schutzbedürftige Auge.

When he looks closely, the observer of the Red Sea butterflyfishes will surely notice that many species are wearing an "eye bandage" such as the yellowedge butterflyfish here. Hidden behind it are always the vulnerable eyes.

Riesenfalterfisch   Giant butterflyfish   *Chaetodon lineolatus*

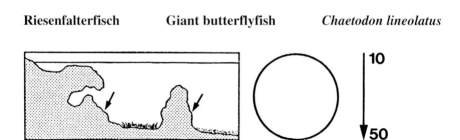

Mit 30 cm Länge ist der Riesenfalterfisch der größte seiner Gattung. Die im Indopazifik weitverbreitete Art ist aber im Roten Meer selten.

With a length of 30 cm, the giant butterflyfish ist the largest in its genus. Although it is the most widespread species in the Indo-Pacific, it is rare in the Red Sea.

Gelbsaumfalterfisch Yellowedge butterflyfish *Chaetodon melannotus*

Riesenfalterfisch Giant butterflyfish *Chaetodon lineolatus*

WIMPELFISCHE

BANNERFISHES

Rotmeerwimpelfisch **Red sea bannerfish** *Heniochus intermedius*
Eckiger Wimpelfisch **Pennant bannerfish** *Heniochus diphreutes*

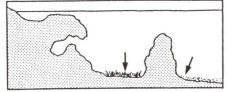

Die zur Falterfischfamilie gehörenden Wimpelfische sind im Roten Meer mit zwei Arten vertreten, wobei der endemische Rotmeerwimpel häufig in Paaren und Schulen (siehe auch Seite 151) im Zwanzigmeterbereich anzutreffen ist. Der seltene Eckige Wimpelfisch nimmt Zooplankton auf, wogegen der Rotmeerwimpel die Nahrung vom Untergrund zupft.

The bannerfishes, part of the butterflyfish family, are represented in the Red Sea by two species. The endemic Red Sea bannerfish is frequently seen in pairs and schools (see also page 151) around the 20 m depth. The rare pennant bannerfish feeds on plankton, whereas the Red Sea bannerfish plucks its food from the bottom.

Rotmeerwimpelfisch Red sea bannerfish *Heniochus intermedius* ▶
Eckiger Wimpelfisch Pennant bannerfish *Heniochus diphreutes*

ROCHEN RAYS
Verschiedene Familien **Various Families**

Rochen gehören zu den Knorpelfischen. Die häufigsten Vertreter der Zitter- und Stechrochen werden in diesem Kapitel vorgestellt, unterteilt in am Boden lebende und zumeist freischwimmende Arten. Oft halb eingegraben, sind sie für den Taucher schwierig zu erkennen. Freischwimmende Rochen werden 300 cm lang.

Rays belong to the cartilaginous fishes. The most common members of the electric rays and stingrays are introduced in this chapter, divided into benthic (bottom dwelling) and pelagic (open sea) species. Often halfway dug into the bottom, they are difficult for the diver to recognize. Open sea rays grow to a length of 300 cm.

Typischer Stechrochen im Roten Meer   Typical Stingray in the Red Sea ▶

Rotmeerzitterrochen   Red sea electric ray   *Torpedo sinuspersici*

ROCHEN   RAYS

Blaupunktrochen   **Bluespotted stingray**   *Taeniura lymma*
Schwarzpunktrochen   **Blackspotted stingray**   *Taeniura meyeni*

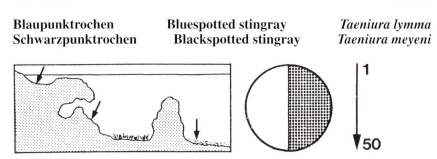

Taucher sollten sich vor dem giftigen Stachel hüten, den Stechrochen auf dem Schwanz tragen. Die abgebildeten Arten graben das Sediment nach Schnecken, Würmern und Krebstieren um.

Divers should beware of the venomous spines which stingrays carry on their tails. The species pictured here grub in the sediment for snails, worms and crustaceans.

Schwarzpunktrochen   Blackspotted stingray   *Taeniura meyeni*

Blaupunktrochen   Bluespotted stingray   *Taeniura lymma*

Schwarzpunktrochen   Blackspotted stingray   *Taeniura meyeni*

ROCHEN   RAYS

| Mantarochen | Manta ray | *Manta ehrenbergii* |

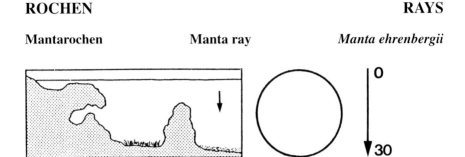

Bewundert in allen Weltmeeren ist die Eleganz der Mantarochen. Wenn sie sich im Februar eines jeden Jahres im Roten Meer zu kleinen Gruppen zusammenschließen, beginnt die Kamerajagd der Unterwasserfotografen.

The elegance of the manta ray is admired in all the seas and oceans. When they gather together in small groups in the Red Sea every February, the underwater photographers begin their camera hunts.

| Adlerrochen | Eagle ray | *Aetobatis narinari* |

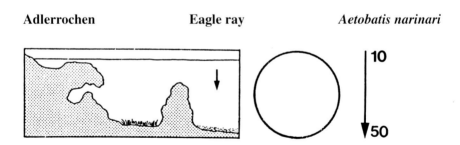

Der populäre Adlerrochen gibt die majestätische Schwimmweise und Erscheinung innerhalb seiner Familie wieder. Wie die Mantas patroullieren Adlerrochen gern vor Dropoffs am Außenriff.

The popular eagle ray possesses the same majestic apperance and swimming movements within his own family. Like the mantas, the eagle rays like to patrol in front ot the dropoffs on the ocean side of the reefs.

Mantarochen Manta ray *Manta ehrenbergii*

Adlerrochen Eagle ray *Aetobatis narinari*

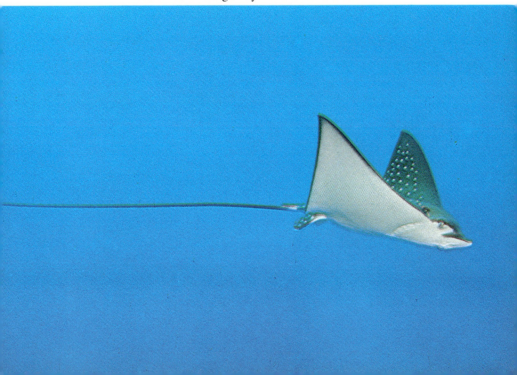

HAIE

Verschiedene Familien

SHARKS

Various Families

Weißspitzenriffhai	Whitetip reef shark	*Triaenodon obesus*
Gepunkteter Ammenhai	Variegated nurse shark	*Stegosoma fasciatum*
Gelbbrauner Ammenhai	Tawny nurse shark	*Nebrius concolor*

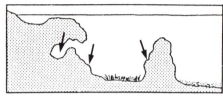 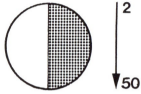

In diesem Kapitel werden riffgebundene und freischwimmende Haie des Roten Meeres gezeigt. Tauchern werden sie grundsätzlich nicht gefährlich, Angriffe auf badende Menschen an den Rotmeerküsten sind aber bekannt geworden. Bis auf den Walhai werden sie max. 350 cm lang.

In this chapter the reef-dwelling as well as the open-sea sharks of the Red Sea are pictured. They are basically not dangerous to divers, although attacks on bathers on the Red Sea coasts have been reported. Exept for the whale shark, they reach a maximum length of 350 cm.

Weißspitzenriffhai   Whitetip reef shark   *Triaenodon obesus*

Gepunkteter Ammenhai Variegated nurse shark *Stegosoma fasciatum*

Gelbbrauner Ammenhai Tawny nurse shark *Nebrius concolor*

HAIE   SHARKS

Arten der Gattung *Carcharhinus* bewegen die Phantasie von Wassersportlern immer wieder. Da durch die Taucherbrille die Fische immer größer aussehen als sie wirklich sind, sei festgestellt, daß keiner der vier abgebildeten Arten länger als 300 cm wird. Die eleganten Dauerschwimmer ernähren sich von Fischen, Cephalopoden und großen Krebstieren. Ausgewachsene Exemplare auch von anderen Haien, Rochen, Schildkröten, Seevögeln und Meeressäugern.

Species of the genus *Carcharhinus* repeatedly arouse the imagination of aquatic sports lovers. Since fish always look larger through a diving mask than they actually are, it should be noted that none of the four species pictured here are larger than 300 cm. These elegant marathon swimmers feed on fishes, cephalopods, and large crustaceans; fully grown specimens also feed on other sharks, rays, turtles, sea birds and mammals.

| **Großrückenflossenhai** | **Big dorsalfin shark** | *Carcharhinus plumbeus* |
| **Schweinsaugenhai** | **Pigeye shark** | *Carcharhinus amboinensis* |

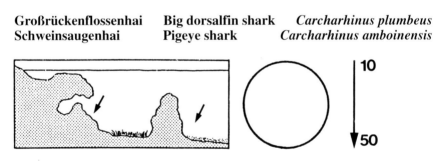

Aus der Adria wurde der in allen Meeren vorkommende Großrückenflossenhai zum erstenmal beschrieben. Auch im Roten Meer lebt er in Riffnähe und frißt mit Vorliebe Tintenfische und Schnecken. Einen sehr gedrungenen Körper besitzt der Schweinsaugenhai, dessen Innenseiten der Brustflossen weiß gerändert sind. Von beiden sind keine Angriffe auf Menschen bekannt.

The big dorsalfin shark, a resident of all the world's seas, was first described in the Adriatic Sea. In the Red Sea it also lives near the reefs and prefers to feed on octopuses and snails. The pigeye shark has a very thickset body, with white margins on the insides of the pectoral fins. Neither species has been known to attack man.

Großrückenflossenhai Big dorsalfin shark *Carcharhinus plumbeus*

Schweinsaugenhai Pigeye shark *Carcharhinus amboinensis*

HAIE

SHARKS

Silberspitzenhai	Silvertip shark	*Carcharhinus albimarginatus*
Grauer Riffhai	Grey reef shark	*Carcharhinus amblyrhynchos*

Im Roten Meer wurde der Silberspitzenhai erstmals nachgewiesen, doch bewohnt er auch weite Teile des Indischen und Pazifischen Ozeans. Außer ihm tragen noch zwei weitere Haiarten auf der ersten Rückenflosse eine kräftige weiße Spitze. Verwechslungen sind eigentlich unter den dreien nicht möglich, wenn man *T. obesus* (Seite 156) betrachtet. Ebenso nicht mit *C. longimanus*, dem Hochsee-Weißspitzenhai. Dessen Rückenflosse ist im Gegensatz zum Silberspitzenhai wie ein Bogen gerundet. Es sind Angriffe des Silberspitzenhais auf Menschen registriert worden.

The silvertip shark has been discovered in the Red Sea for the first time, but it inhabits wide stretches of the Indian and Pacific Oceans. Two other species besides this one have prominent white tips on their first dorsal fins. Mix-ups among the three are actually not possible when one takes a close look at *T. obesus* (page 156) and *C. longimanus*, the pelagic whitetip shark, whose dorsal fin is rounded like an arch, in contrast to that of the silvertip. Attacks on man by silvertip sharks have been recorded.

Der graue Riffhai ist wohl der häufigste Hai im Indischen Ozean neben dem bereits vorgestellten *T. obesus* (Seite 156). Auch wenn er im Roten Meer in Küstennähe nicht rudelartig gesehen wird wie um die Malediven, wo er in Dressurakte wie Hand- und Mundfütterungen durch Taucher einbezogen ist, so begegnet man ihm hier regelmäßig an Dropoffs, wo das Wasser auch klar ist. Obwohl es im gesamten Verbreitungsgebiet dieser Art leichte Farbunterschiede gibt und verschiedene Wissenschaftler deshalb andere Namen benutzen, erscheint der Name des erstbeschriebenen Grauen Riffhais, *C. amblyrhynchos*, nach wie vor gültig. Obwohl diese Art nicht länger als 180 cm wird, sind Angriffe auf Menschen bekannt geworden.

The grey reef shark is probably the most numerous shark in the Indian Ocean after the aforementioned *T. obesus* (page 156). In the Red Sea they are not found in packs as is the case around the Maldives, where they have been trained and included in acts where they eat out of a diver's hand. In the Red Sea they are regularly encountered at dropoffs, where the water is also clear. Although this species has some slight colour differences in different parts of its range, the name used for the first official description of the grey reef shark, *C. amblyrhynchos*, appears still to be valid. Attacks on humans have been known, although this species is no longer than 180 cm.

Silberspitzenhai   Silvertip shark   *Carcharhinus albimarginatus*

Grauer Riffhai   Grey reef shark   *Carcharhinus amblyrhynchos*

HAIE

SHARKS

Gekerbter Hammerhai   Scalloped hammerhead   *Sphyrna lewini*
Walhai   Whaleshark   *Rhincodon typus*

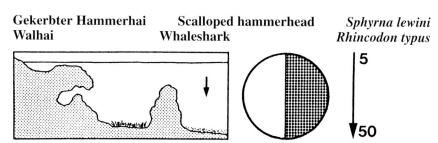

Von der Familie der Hammerhaie mit ihrer ungewöhnlichen Kopfform ist der gekerbte Hammerhai, *S. lewini*, noch der verbreitetste. Wissenschaftler nehmen an, daß der Kopf der besseren Manövrierfähigkeit dient. Zudem dürften Hammerhaie wegen der weit auseinanderstehenden Augen und Naseneingänge besser und schneller sehen oder auf andere Weise Beute wahrnehmen. Taucher fahren gern an die sudanesische Küste, weil diese Art dort regelmäßig in Rudeln auftritt. Ihre Hauptnahrung besteht aus Tintenfisch (Sepien, Kalmare), Angriffe auf Menschen sind nicht bekannt geworden.

S. lewini is still the most widespread member of the hammerhead shark family, whose members have such an unusual head shape. Scientists assume that this head shape promotes better maneuverability. In addition, because of their widely separated eyes and nostrils, the hammerhead sharks should be able to see otherwise perceive their prey better and more quickly. Interested divers like to go to the Sudanese coast, as this species regularly appears in packs there. Feed primarily on squid and cuttlefish. Attacks on humans are unknown.

Wenn man wie ich bei seinem dritten Rotmeertauchgang überhaupt gleich zwei zusammenschwimmenden Walhaien begegnet, sich von ihnen an der Schwanzflosse hängend durch riesige Krebsschwärme ziehen läßt, so bewirkt das sicher einen bleibenden Eindruck. Der max. 14 m lange Walhai ist der größte Fisch der Erde und schwimmt in offenem Wasser. Er ist Planktonfresser und für Menschen ungefährlich.

It a diver were to encounter right away, as I did on my third Red Sea dive, a pair of whale sharks swimming together, and wereto hitch a ride on a tail fin through huge swarms of crustaceans, that would certainly leave a lasting impression. With a maximum length of 14 m, the whale shark is the largest fish on earth, and swims in the open sea. It feeds on plankton and is harmless to humans.

Gekerbter Hammerhai Scalloped hammerhead *Sphyrna lewini*

Walhai Whaleshark *Rhincodon typus*

INDEX DEUTSCH
INDEX GERMAN

A
Abudjubbes Lippfisch 62
Achtlinienlippfisch 72
Adlerrochen 154
Anemonenfische 44
Anglerfische 94
Arabischer Kaiserfisch 130
Augenfleckmirakelbarsch 54

B
Barakudas 106
Barben 56
Bärtiger Drachenkopf 90
Baskenmützenzackenbarsch 40
Besenschwanzlippfisch 62
Blauer Segelflossendoktor 26
Blauer Drücker 118
Blauflossenmakrele 104
Blauklingendoktorfisch 34
Blaupunktrochen 152
Blauschuppenschnapper 110
Blaustreifenseenadel 84
Blitzlichtfische 100
Blutflecken-Husar 128
Brassen 112
Brauner Segelflossendoktor 26
Brauner Doktorfisch 28
Braunfleckenzackenbarsch 40
Buckelkopfpapageienfisch 74
Büschelbarsche 52

D
Dianas Lippfisch 70
Dickkopfmakrele 104
Doktorfische 24
Dorniges Seepferdchen 84
Drückerfische 114

E
Eckiger Wimpelfisch 148
Eidechsenfische 94
Einfleckschnapper 108

F
Fähnchenfalterfisch 144
Fahnenbarsche 48
Falterfische 138
Familie Balistidae 114
Familie Labridae 60
Familie Acanthuridae 24
Familie Mullidae 56
Familie Sphyraenidae 106
Familie Carangidae 102
Familie Labridae 68
Familie Muraenidae 78
Familie Chaetodontidae 138
Familie Pomacanthidae 130
Familie Serranidae 36
Familie Scaridae 74
Familie Scorpaenidae 88
Familie Tetraodontidae 120
Feilenfische 98
Fetzengeisterfisch 86
Fledermausfische 98
Flötenfische 96
Flügelroßfische 92
Forsskal Barbe 58
Forsters Büschelbarsch 52
Fridmans Zwergbarsch 50
Füsiliere 112

G
Gekerbter Hammerhai 162
Gelbbrauner Ammenhai 156
Gelbklingendoktorfisch 32
Gelbsattelbarbe 56
Gelbsaumfalterfisch 146
Gelbschwanzdrücker 114
Gepunkteter Ammenhai 156
Graue Muräne 90

Grauer Riffhai 160
Großaugenmakrele 102
Großaugenschnapper 110
Großaugenbarsch 128
Große Lippfische 60
Großer Barrakuda 106
Großrückenflossenhai 158
Großschulenbarbe 58
Großschulenbarrakuda 106
Großzahnlippfisch 68
Grüner Riffbarsch 46

H
Haie 156
Halbmondkaiserfisch 132
Haremsfahnenbarsch 48
Heemstrafahnenbarsch 48

I
Imperatorkaiser 130

J
Juwelenzackenbarsch 40

K
Kaiserfische 130
Kleine Lippfische 68
Kleine Barsche 44
Kofferfische 100
Krokodilfische 92
Kronenkugelfisch 120
Kugelfische 120
Kurzflossenfeuerfisch 88
Kurznasendoktor 34

L
Langnasenbüschelbarsch 52
Langnasendoktorfisch 32
Leopardenzackenbarsch 42
Lyrakaiserfisch 134
Lyraschwanz-Lippfisch 68

M
Malabarzackenbarsch 36
Mantarochen 154
Maskenfalterfisch 138
Maskenkugelfisch 122
Mirakelbarsche 54
Mondflossenzackenbarsch 40
Mondschwanz-
Lippfisch 70
Muränen 78

N
Napoleon-Lippfisch 60

O
Olivenzwergbarsch 50
Orangenfleckmakrele 104
Orangenkopffalterfisch 144

P
Papageienfische 74
Pfauenkaiserfisch 134
Pfeifenfische 82
Polypenfalterfisch 142
Preußenfisch 46

R
Riesendrücker 116
Riesenmuräne 78
Riesenhusar 126
Riffbarsche 46
Rochen 150
Rostpapageifisch 76
Rotbrustlippfisch 62
Rotfeuerfisch 88
Rotfleckfalterfisch 142
Rotmaulzackenbarsch 38
Rotmeeranemonenfisch 44
Rotmeerigelfisch 124
Rotmeerpicassodrücker 118
Rotmeerputzerlippfisch 72
Rotmeerrauchkaiser 136

Rotmeerwimpelfisch 148
Rotmeerzitterrochen 150
Rotmeerzwergkaiser 136
Rotzahndrücker 116
Rüppells Muräne 80

S
Schachbrettlippfisch 66
Schnapper 108
Schneeflockenmuräne 80
Schultz' Seenadel 82
Schwarzbrustseenadel 82
Schwarzer Doktorfisch 28
Schwarzfleckkugelfisch 124
Schwarzgepunktete Süßlippe 110
Schwarzweißschnapper 108
Schweinsaugenhai 158
Seegrasgeisterfisch 86
Seifenbarsche 54
Silberspitzenhai 160
Silberstrich-Barrakuda 106
Skorpionsfische 88
Sohaldoktorfisch 30
Soldatenfische 126
Spiegelfleck-Lippfisch 66
Springers Zwergbarsch 50
Stachelmakrelen 102
Stechrochen 150
Steinfisch 90
Strahlenfeuerfisch 88
Streifenfahnenbarsch 48
Stülpmaul-Lippfisch 64
Summanazackenbarsch 42

T
Tabakfalterfisch 140
Teppich-Krokodilsfisch 92
Torpedomakrele 102

W
Walhai 162
Wangenbandlippfisch 64
Weißfleckkugelfisch 122
Weißschwanzflossendrücker 118
Weißspitzenriffhai 156
Welse 96
Wimpelfische 148

Z
Zackenbarsche 36
Zweifleckschnapper 108
Zwergbarsche 50
Zwergkugelfisch 120

INDEX ENGLISCH
INDEX ENGLISH

A
Abudjubbe's wrasse 62
Anemonefishes 44
Angelfish 130
Arabian angelfish 130

B
Bandcheck wrasse 64
Bandet damsel 46
Bannerfish 148
Barracuda 106
Basslets 44
Batfish 98
Bearded dragonshead 90
Big head jack 104
Big wrasses 60
Big dorsalfin shark 158
Bigeye snapper 110
Bigeye jack 102
Bigeye 128
Bigtooth wrasse 68
Black tang 28
Black and white snapper 108
Blackchest pipefish 82
Blackspotted puffer 124
Blackspotted stingray 152
Blackspotted sweetlip 110
Blacktip grouper 40
Blue trigger 118
Blue sailfintang 26
Bluefin jack 104
Bluescale snapper 110
Bluespinetang 34
Bluespotted stingray 152
Bluestripe pipefish 84
Boxfish 100

Breams 112
Bristletoothtang 28
Broomtail wrasse 62
Brown tang 28
Brown sailfintang 26
Butterflyfish 138

C
Checkerboard wrasse 66
Chevron barracuda 106
Clearfin turkeyfish 88
Comet basslet 54
Cornetfish 96
Crescent angelfish 132
Crownpuffer 120

D
Damselfish 46
Devil basslets 54
Diana's wrasse 70
Doublebar bream 112
Doublespot wrasse 66
Dwarfpuffer 120

E
Eagle ray 154
Eel catfish 96
Eightline wrasse 72
Emperor angelfish 130

F
Filefish 98
Flag basslet 48
Flashlight fish 100
Flathead 92
Forsskal's goatfish 58
Fridman's pygmy basslet 50
Frogfish 94
Fusilier 112

G
Giant grouper   38
Giant butterflyfish   146
Giant moray   78
Giant squirrelfish   126
Goatfish   56
Goldband fusilier   112
Goldstriped soapfish   54
Greasy grouper   40
Great barracuda   106
Green damsel   46
Grey reef shark   160
Grey moray   806
Groupers   36

H
Harem flag basslet   48
Hawkfishes   52
Heemstra flag basslet   48

J
Jacks   102
Jewelgrouper   40

L
Leopard grouper   42
Lizardfish   94
Longnose hawkfish   52
Longnosetang   32
Lunartail grouper   34
Lyre angelfish   134
Lyretail wrasse   68

M
Malabar grouper   36
Manta ray   154
Masked butterflyfish   138
Masked puffer   122
Moontail wrasse   70
Moray   78

N
Napoleon wrasse   60

O
Olive pygmy basslet   50
Onespot snapper   108
Orangeface butterflyfish   144
Orangespotted jack   104

P
Parrotfish   74
Pennant bannerfish   148
Pigeye shark   158
Pipefish   82
Polyp butterflyfish   142
Pygmy basslet   50

R
Racoon butterflyfish   140
Rag ghost pipefish   86
Rays   150
Red sea anemonefish   44
Red sea bannerfish   148
Red sea burrfish   124
Red sea cleaner wrasse   72
Red sea dwarfangelfish   136
Red sea electric ray   150
Red sea picasso trigger   118
Red sea smoke angelfish   136
Red turkeyfish   88
Redback butterflyfish   142
Redbreasted wrasse   62
Redmouth grouper   38
Redtoothtrigger   116
Royal angelfish   134
Rüppell's moray   80
Rusty parrotfish   76

S
Scalloped hammerhead 162
Schooling barracuda 106
Schooling goatfish 58
Schultz' pipefish 82
Scorpionfishes 88
Seagras ghost pipefish 86
Seamoth 92
Shark 156
Shortfin turkeyfish 88
Shortnosetang 34
Silvertip shark 160
Small wrasses 68
Snappers 108
Snowflake moray 80
Soapfishes 54
Soldierfish 126
Springer's pygmy basslet 52
Steepheaded parrotfish 74
Stingray 150
Stonefish 90
Striped flag basslet 48
Summana grouper 42
Surgeonfish 24

T
Tang 24
Tawny nurse shark 156
Thorny seahorse 84
Threadfin butterflyfish 144
Titantrigger 116
Torpedo jack 102
Torpedo squirrelfish 128
Triggerfish 114
Twinspot snapper 108

V
Variegated nurse shark 156

W
Whaleshark 162
Whitespotted puffer 122
Whitetail trigger 118
Whitetip reef shark 156

Y
Yellowedge butterflyfish 146
Yellowsaddle goatfish 56
Yellowspinetang 32
Yellowtail trigger 114

INDEX WISSENSCHAFTLICH
INDEX SCIENTIFIC

A
Acanthopagrus bifasciatus 112
Acanthurinae 24
Acanthurus gahhm 28
Acanthurus nigrofuscus 28
Acanthurus sohal 30
Aethaloperca rogaa 38
Aetobatis narinari 154
Amphiprion bicinctus 44
Anomalopidae 100
Antennariidae 94
Anthiidae 48
Apolemichtyhs xanthotis 136
Arothron stellatus 124
Arothron hispidus 122
Arothron diadematus 122

B
Balistapus undulatus 114
Balistidae 114
Balistoides viridescens 116
Bodianus anthioides 68
Bodianus diana 70

C
Caesionidae 112
Calloplesiops altivelis 54
Canthigaster coronata 120
Canthigaster pygmaea 120
Carangoides bajad 104
Caranx ignobilis 104
Caranx melampygus 104
Caranx sexfasciatus 102
Carcharhinus albimarginatus 160
Carcharhinus plumbeus 158
Carcharhinus amblyrhyncos 160
Carcharhinus amboinensis 158
Centropyge multispinis 136
Cephalopholis miniata 40
Chaetodon paucifasciatus 142
Chaetodon auriga 144
Chaetodon austriacus 142
Chaetodon fasciatus 140
Chaetodon lineolatus 146
Chaetodon larvatus 144
Chaetodon semilarvatus 138
Chaetodon melannotus 146
Chaetodontidae 138
Cheilinus lunulatus 62
Cheilinus undulatus 60
Cheilinus abudjubbe 62
Cheilinus fasciatus 62
Cheilinus digrammus 64
Chilomycteris spilostylus 124
Chromis viridis 46
Cirrhitidae 52
Coris aygula 66
Corythoichthys nigripectus 82
Corythoichthys schultzi 82
Ctenochaetus striatus 28

D
Dascyllus aruanus 46
Dendrochirus brachypterus 88
Doryrhampus excisus 84

E
Echidua nebulosa 80
Ephippidae 98
Epibulus insidiator 64
Epinephelus malabaricus 36
Epinephelus summana 42
Epinephelus fasciatus 40
Epinephelus tauvina 40
Epinephelus tukula 38
Eurypegasus draconis 92

F
Fistularia commersonii 96
Fistulariidae 96
G
Genicanthus caudovitattus 134
Grammistes sexlineatus 54
Grammistidae 54
Gymnothorax rueppelliae 80
Gymnothorax javanicus 78

H
Halichoeres hortulanus 66
Heniochus diphreutes 148
Heniochus intermedius 148
Hippocampus histrix 84

L
Labridae 60
Larabicus quadrilineatus 72
Lethrinus nebulosus 110
Lutjanus bohar 108
Lutjanus monostigma 108

M
Macolor niger 108
Manta ehrenbergii 154
Marcopharyngodon bipartitus 68
Monacanthidae 98
Monotaxis grandoculis 110
Mullidae 56
Mulloidichtys vanicolensis 58
Muraenidae 78

N
Naso hexacanthus 34
Naso unicornis 34
Naso lituratus 34
Naso brevirostris 32
Nebrius concolor 156
Neoniphon sammara 128

O
Odonus niger 116
Ostraciidae 100
Ostracion cubicus 100
Oxycirrhites typus 52

P
Papilloculiaps longiceps 92
Paracirrhites forsteri 52
Paracheilinus octotaenia 72
Parupeneus cyclostomus 56
Platycephalidae 92
Plectorhynchus gaterinus 110
Plectropomus marisrubi 42
Plesiopidae 54
Plotosidae 96
Photoblepharon Steinitzi 100
Pomacanthidae 130
Pomacanthus asfur 132
Pomacanthus imperator 130
Pomacanthus maculosus 130
Pomacentridae 44
Pseudanthias squamipinnis 48
Pseudanthias heemstrai 48
Pseudanthias taeniatus 48
Pseudobalistes fuscus 118
Pseudochromidae 50
Pseudochromis springeri 50
Pseudochromis fridmani 50
Pseudochromis olivacei 50
Pterois volitans 88
Pterois radiata 88
Pterocaesio chrysozona 112
Pygolites diacanthus 134

R
Rhincodon typus 162
Rhinecanthus assasi 118

S
Sargocentron spinifer 126
Scaridae 74

Scarus gibbus 74
Scarus ferrugineus 76
Scomberoides lysan 102
Scorpaenidae 88
Scorpaenopsis barbatus 90
Serranidae 36
Siderea grisea 80
Solenostomous paradoxus 86
Solenostomus cyanopterus 86
Sparidae 112
Sphyraena quenie 106
Sphyraena barracuda 106
Sphyraena jello 106
Sphyraenidae 106
Sphyrna lewini 162
Stegosoma fasciatum 156
Sufflamen albicaudatus 118
Synanceia verrucosa 90
Syndontidae 94

T
Taeniura meyeni 152
Taeniura lymma 152
Tetraodontidae 120
Thalassoma lunare 70
Torpedo sp. 150
Triaenodon obesus 156

V
Variola louti 36

Z
Zebrasoma desjardini 26
Zebrasoma xanthurum 26

BILDNACHWEIS • PHOTO CREDIT
Fischführer Rotes Meer • Red Sea Fishguide
(Reihenfolge der Fotografen nach der Häufigkeit der Bilder, oben/above = o., unten/below = u., i = insert)

Helmut Debelius: 25, 27 o., 27 u., 29 o., 29 u., 31, 31 o. i., 33 o., 33 o. 2xi, 33 u., 34, 35 u., 35 o., 37 o., 40, 45, 47 u., 48, 48 i, 49 o., 49 u., 50, 51 o., 51 u., 53 u., 55 o., 55 u., 56, 57, 60, 62, 65 o., 65 u., 67 o. i, 67 u. i, 69 o., 69 o. i, 69 u., 69 u. i, 71 o., 71 o. i, 71 u. i, 73 o., 73 u., 75 u., 76, 77 u., 78, 81 o., 81 u., 83 o., 85 o., 87 o., 88, 89 u., 90, 91 o., 93 u., 95 o., 97 u., 97 u. i, 99 o., 101 o., 102, 103 u., 105 u., 107 u., 108, 109 u., 111 o., 113 u., 117 u., 118, 119 o., 119 u., 121 o. + u., 123 o., 124 o., 127 o., 129 u., 131 o. i, 132, 133 u., 135 o., i, 135 u., 137 o., 137 u., 141 u. i, 143 o., 143 u.i, 145 o., 145 u., 147 o., 148, 150, 151, 153 o., 154 u., 156, 161 o., 163 u. **Marwan El-Dewey:** Luftaufnahme S. 23. **Rolf Schmidt:** 37 u., 41 o., 59 u., 61, 77 o., 93 o., 103 o., 104, 110, 115, 117 o., 127 u., 139 o., 147 u., 153 u., 154 o., 157 o. **Norbert Probst:** 28, 39 o., 41 u., 42, 53 o., 63 o., 79, 80, 83 o., 89 o., 105 o., 107 o., 109 o., 111 u., 122, 123 u., 149. **Wolfgang Fiedler:** 63 u., 75 o., 81 u. i, 85 u., 113 o., 139 u. **Andrea Ghisotti:** 71 u., 99 u., 125 u., 152, 161 u., 163 o. **Elke Bärmann:** 43 o., 43 u., 91 u., 97 o., 131 u. **Dr. Jankees Post:** 67 u., 101 u., 141 o., 159 o. **John Neuschwander:** 31 u. i, 47 o., 67 o., 131 o., **Dr. Gerald Allen:** 131 u. i, 133 o., 133 u. i, **Klaus Hilgert:** 39 u., 97 o. i, 157 u. **Dr. Friedrich Naglschmid:** 59 o., 81 u. i, 143 o. **Matthias Haffner:** 86. **Dieter Hengst:** 159 u. **Tony Holm:** 87 u. **Inge Lenmark:** 106.

Das gesamte Bildmaterial entstammt dem Unterwasser-Archiv IKAN.
All of the photographic material was drawnfrom the underwater-archive IKAN.

LITERATURVERZEICHNIS • BIBLIOGRAPHY
Fischführer Rotes Meer • Red Sea Fishguide

ALLEN, Gerald: Butterfly and angelfishes of the world, Mergus Verlag 1979. DEBELIUS, Helmut: Gepanzerte Meeresritter/Armoured knights of the sea, Kernen Verlag 1983. DEBELIUS, Helmut: Fischpartner Niederer Tiere/ Colourful little reef fishes, Hobbing Verlag 1986. DEBELIUS, Helmut: Fischführer Indischer Ozean, Tetra 1993. EICHLER, D. + LIESKE, E.: Korallenfische Indischer Ozean, Jahr-Verlag 1994. FRICKE, Hans: Bericht aus dem Riff, Piper Verlag 1976. GÖTHEL, Helmut: Farbatlas Meeresfauna. Rotes Meer, Indischer Ozean (Malediven)-Fische, Ulmer 1994. GOHAR, H. + MAZHAR, F.: Publ. Marine Biol. Station Al-Ghardaqa Nr. 13, Cairo University Press 1964. HANSEN, Thorkild: Reise nach Arabien, Hoffmann und Campe Verlag 1965. KLAUSEWITZ, Wolfgang: E. Rüppell zum 100. Todestag, Natur und Museum 1984. KLAUSEWITZ, Wolfgang: Fische aus dem Roten Meer, Senck. biol. 1959. LIESKE, E. + MYERS, R. F.: Korallenfische der Welt, Jahr-Verlag 1994. MASUDA, Hajime: Fieldguide Fishes, Tokai University Press 1984. MERGNER, H. and SCHUHMACHER, H.: Morphologie, Ökologie und Zonierung von Korallenriffen bei Aqaba, Helgoländer wiss. Meeresunters. 26, 238-358, 1974. NEUBAUER, Wilbert: Korallenfische im Aquarium, Kosmos Verlag 1973. NIEBUHR, Carsten: Entdeckungen im Orient, Erdmann Verlag, Tübingen 1973. PATZNER, Robert + DEBELIUS, Helmut: Partnerschaft im Meer, Pfriem Verlag 1984. RANDALL, John: Red Sea Reef Fishes, Immel Publishing 1983. RANDALL, John: Sharks of Arabia, Immel Publishing 1986. RÜPPEL, Eduard: Atlas zu der Reise im nördlichen Afrika, Senckenberg Museum 1828–30. SCHMID, Peter + PASCHKE, Dietmar: Unterwasserführer Rotes Meer – Niedere Tiere, Verlag Naglschmid 1986. SMITH, Margret + HEEMSTRA, Philipp: Smith's Sea Fishes, Springer Verlag 1986.